GIANTS

OF THE

CLYDE

By the same author:

Scotland's Cruel Sea
Peterhead: the Inside Story of Scotland's Toughest Prison
Gentle Johnny Ramensky
The Barlinnie Story
A Boxing Dynasty: The Tommy Gilmour Story
(with Tommy Gilmour)
Real Hard Cases: True Crime from the Streets
(with Les Brown)
Glasgow's Godfather
Gangs of Glasgow
Glasgow Crimefighter: The Les Brown Story (with Les Brown)
Glasgow's Hard Men
Blood on the Streets: The A-Z of Glasgow Crime
The Wee Book of Glasgow
The Wee Book of the Clyde
Crimes Past: Glasgow's Crimes of the Century

Co-authored with Ian Watson:

Clydeside People and Places
The Herald Book of the Clyde
Doon the Watter
Scotland's Sporting Heroes
Images of Glasgow

GIANTS
OF THE
CLYDE

The Great Ships and the Great Yards

Robert Jeffrey

BLACK & WHITE PUBLISHING

First published 2017
by Black & White Publishing Ltd
29 Ocean Drive, Edinburgh EH6 6JL

1 3 5 7 9 10 8 6 4 2   17 18 19 20

ISBN: 978 1 78530 074 5

A CIP catalogue record for this book is available from the British Library.

Typeset by Iolaire, Newtonmore
Printed and bound by CPI Group (UK) Ltd., Croydon, CR0 4YY

Contents

Acknowledgements

Ian Bruce, Tom Bone, Sammy Gilmore, Albert Smart, Ronald Ross, Ray Bulloch, Scott Whiteford, staff of Mitchell Library, staff of Denny Ship Tank Museum, staff of Scottish Maritime Museum Irvine, Dr Grant Jeffrey, Dr Stuart Jeffrey, Marie Jeffrey, Jim Campbell, Stuart Irvine, John Riddell, Jim Williamson, Ian McAdam, Stuart Fyfe, David Frost, Lise Jeffrey. And many old timers who worked in the yards, sailed on the vessels and loved to talk of the Clyde.

Giants of the Clyde is dedicated to Alex Jeffrey, freethinker, music maker and Clyde enthusiast.

Introduction

This book makes no wild claims to be comprehensive – to do so would call for many volumes and many years spent scouring around in dusty archives. Instead it is an occasionally personal, and perhaps idiosyncratic, selection of tales that appeal to a life-long Clydesider, just one of a huge tribe of "boat daft" Scots of all ages who have lived near the river. In it are stories of famous ships and the yards, large and small, that built them, that hopefully give something of the flavour of a unique place and its peoples, the folk who made the ships that made a mark on the world.

Smoke, Noise, Clamour, Clatter and the Ding Dong of Hammer on Metal

It all began in earnest around 1796 with the opening of the Monkland Canal which provided Glasgow with good access to the iron ore and coal mines of Lanarkshire. At the same time the Clyde itself began to be dredged and deepened allowing shipbuilding almost in the city centre, in Govan on the south bank and with yards like Yarrow's and A. & J. Inglis on the north. It was the start of one of the most fascinating and life transforming episodes in industrial history – the birth of a legend, and an accolade that became around the world a byword for supreme maritime craftsmanship, "Clydebuilt".

Today a couple of existing replica ships – one at Port Glasgow and the other an exhibit on the Monkland Canal itself – mark important episodes in shipbuilding history. Twenty-three years after the opening of the canal what some say is the world's first iron-hulled boat was built at Calderbank in Lanarkshire. This was the iron riveted *Vulcan* and its success helped kick-start a shipbuilding revolution on the Clyde. But in its early days *Vulcan*'s design was too much for the local barge men, soaked in the history and traditions of wooden hulls, to handle. They mocked it as a false dawn and some even predicted that it would never float! But the 63-feet horse-drawn barge, named after the Roman god of fire, was a success, working on the Forth and Clyde canal for more than fifty years ferrying coal, ironstone and passengers. A replica was built for the Glasgow Garden Festival in 1988 and for a time was a feature of the Summerlee Museum of Scottish Industrial Life in Coatbridge.

Another replica that is a must-visit for anyone with an interest in the Clyde's history and its effect on the development of shipping worldwide is that of the *Comet*. This little vessel ran the first commercially successful steamboat service in Europe in August 1812. The replica, which makes industrial Port Glasgow an unlikely attraction for tourists, was constructed in 1962 by shipyard apprentices to mark the 150th anniversary of its historic first voyage.

Not even the most enthusiastic residents could claim that Port Glasgow is easy on the eye. Indeed the replica, which has been kept in excellent condition for more than fifty years, is in a frankly shabby and decaying town centre surrounded by a petrol station, a shopping complex, a motorway, and industrial units. However, the display itself is well done and a credit to an unpretentious working town. The view in the winter and spring across the river to the snow-flecked "Arrochar Alps" and Ben Lomond is impressive, if you can ignore the immediate surroundings.

Many an industrial or maritime landmark is graced with a tiny plaque explaining little to the visitor. Not so in the case of the *Comet*. There is a lot of information placed next to the little black and red vessel, especially a handsome steel tablet full of interesting facts. The giants of the river that came from Port Glasgow and shipyards up and down the Clyde, to the very centre of Glasgow, may have dwarfed this little steamship, but it was undoubtedly the start of something very big indeed.

The steel tablet explains the background to the construction of the *Comet* although it does not point out the interesting fact that the choice of name for the vessel reflects the astronomical sight of the year of its birth, 1811 – a spectacular comet that dominated the night sky for more than a year. The remarkable man with the big idea of building a commercial passenger steamer to ply the Clyde was Henry Bell who owned a hotel and swimming baths in Helensburgh (to be seen across the river from where the replica now lies).

Some think that the idea of the *Comet* came from a little steam engine that Bell had installed to pump seawater into the swimming baths. Like all true entrepreneurs Bell was on the lookout to develop his enterprises and make more money. He had been in contact with the famous engineer Robert Fulton and was interested in steam-propelled boats. Wherever the notion for a passenger steamship came from, Bell chose wisely when he looked for a builder. In John and Charles Wood, of John Wood & Company, the Port Glasgow shipbuilders, he found a company with an enviable reputation for quality work in the sailing ship trade. In 1811 work began on a tiny paddle-powered steam vessel, just 45-feet long with a beam of 10 feet. The funnel for the steam engine was tall and narrow and served to carry a sail which in favourable winds – the engine was of only four horse power – would aid speed and save coal.

As you wander round the replica most people remark on the twin sets of paddles on each side since one large set was the norm in the heyday of the Clyde paddlers. Interestingly, later in its career the actual *Comet* was retro fitted with larger twin sets of paddles, one starboard, one port. There were two small cabin spaces where passengers could sit protected from the weather. Bell had a lot of style and you can't help but reflect that he would have done well in these days of social media. He knew how to spread the word about his enterprises. In August 1812 Bell advertised in a local newspaper *The Greenock Advertiser*:

> The Steamboat Comet between Glasgow, Greenock and Helensburgh for Passengers Only. The subscriber, having at much expense, fitted up a handsome vessel to ply upon the River Clyde from Glasgow, to sail by the power of air, wind, and steam, intends that the vessel shall leave the Broomielaw on Tuesdays, Thursdays, and Saturdays about mid-day, or such hour thereafter as may answer from the state of the tide, and to leave Greenock on Mondays, Wednesdays, and Fridays in the morning to suit the tide.

The fare was "four shillings for the best cabin and three shillings for the second". In 1812 a delivery voyage upriver from Port Glasgow was made, more than 20 miles, and on return she sailed down to Greenock and, despite a headwind, managed a respectable five miles an hour. And so began the long tradition of pleasure steamers linking the sea lochs of the Firth of Clyde and the tourist attractions of towns like Campbeltown, Inveraray, Dunoon, Largs and Rothesay.

Perhaps more importantly it was a modest, if groundbreaking, start to steam-shipbuilding. At its peak in the early years of the twentieth century the riverbanks, north and south, were thronged with cranes, slipways, dry docks, fabrication sheds, furnaces, engine works and design offices. The great yards provided work for thousands of highly skilled men – and a few pioneering women like the rivet catchers who worked alongside men during the pressures of the Second World War. There was smoke, noise, clamour, chatter and clatter and the ding dong of hammer on metal and gentle countryside was turned into a classic industrial scene.

All very different from the birthplace of the Clyde itself many miles upriver in Lanarkshire. There is good-natured scholarly dispute about the actual site of the source and indeed I believe, with many, that there is not one spot which can be identified as the place the Clyde begins. But take a trip up the riverbank to the gentle green hills around Elvanfoot and look up the Daer Valley. On a fine day in spring or summer it is an uplifting rural scene. From these hills runs the water that flows in various springs, including the Daer, the Potrail, and Clyde's Burn, into a river worthy of the name Clyde. As the waters flow west towards the open Atlantic they grow faster and wider with each mile of the journey, through the centre to Glasgow down to the opening firth towards Dumbarton, Helensburgh, Port Glasgow, Greenock and Gourock.

In *The Herald Book of the Clyde* I wrote that physically the Clyde is not a mighty river. It is no Amazon or Mississippi. All the more remarkable that its name resonates worldwide.

2

Billowing Sails, Tea Races and Weel Done, Cutty Sark!

Some phrases from your schooldays stick in the mind throughout your life. Growing up on Clydeside for me it was "Glasgow made the Clyde and the Clyde made Glasgow". But many of the yards whose names are linked with Scotland's greatest industrial city are miles from the centre of the "dear green place" of ancient history (a reference to the area's pleasant valleys and gentle hills before the scenic blight of large-scale industrialisation). However, in passing it is worth mentioning that the decline of shipbuilding has been accompanied with a massive growth in tourism and a flourishing arts scene, so much so that Glasgow is considered by some experts to be one of the world's top tourist cities! Changed days, but the denizens of the city and those in many of the towns on the riverbanks retain a proud folk memory of the great days of the past. Both in the diminishing yards still at work and around sites where great ships were once built but are now, at times, unsightly wastelands there is still a fierce local pride. One such place is Dumbarton where that old saying about the

Clyde that remains in my mind to this day appears in a slightly different version: Denny's made Dumbarton and Dumbarton made Denny's.

The reference is, of course, to the birthplace of such famous ships as the *Cutty Sark*, the American riverboat *Delta Queen*, the pioneering roll on-roll off ferry *Princess Victoria* (to sink in tragic circumstances in the Irish Sea in the fifties) and even seaplanes and hovercraft, for Denny's was perhaps the most innovative of the great yards.

The yard's experimental work on propeller design, for example, led to an early design for a helicopter though it was hardly what you would call a commercial success. Like many another shipbuilders, Denny's (more formally known as William Denny Brothers), finally ran out of steam, as it were, and work dried up in 1963. Now it is a derelict sad sight near Dumbarton Football Club's modern little stadium in the shadow of Dumbarton Rock and its ancient castle. But one tangible reminder of the great days remains, a most remarkable nautical museum, certainly one of the most interesting on the Clyde, in the form of Denny's design offices which escaped destruction. (Fairfield's, further up river and on the opposite bank, also has a fine museum).

The design offices at Denny's were unusual in that they were separate from the yard itself, a few hundred yards away from the river. This part of the yard survived the wrecker's ball that cleared the actual site where the ships were built. The old varnished brown desks of the naval architects, polished and gleaming, are on view, pencils still sharpened and drawing instruments neatly piled ready for use. The walls are thick with photographs of old vessels, finished and under construction. Some famous, some now forgotten. The boardroom where vital financial decisions were taken lies as if ready to spring into action again at a moment's notice. It is not hard to imagine douce waitresses in black and white slipping around the table serving a wee dry sherry here and a large whisky there as the yard's plans were discussed. There are noticeboards on the walls advertising staff events. And many, many fading snaps of after-hours outings enjoyed by the men and women who worked there. The Denny family had a great relationship with the staff and were more than just pioneers in technical matters, they led the way on the Clyde in the employment of women. Perhaps it was my overactive imagination but I took away from my many visits to the museum a feeling that this particular yard had been a happy place to work. Incidentally staff at the museum, led when I visited it by the enthusiastic and knowledgeable Anne Hoben, a woman whose love of the place was obvious, seem to share a spirit of enjoyment in their work.

All shipyards have stories of workplace humour, tales of apprentices sent on errands for parts like "circular iron squares" that did not exist and suchlike. I liked one of the tales of the old days at Denny's in particular – some of the draughtsmen had a sneaky arrangement for a fly cuppa that they thought would fool the bosses. The idea was that if the phone rang a certain number of times but was not answered, then the refreshments were on the way. One day one of the gaffers was talking to a worker when the phone rang. After a few seconds: "That will be your tea," said the boss without a hint of a smile. In a similar vein is the story of Sir Maurice Denny, a good natured and much liked member of the owning family. He liked to drop into the work areas at short notice. But he seldom took the workers by surprise. When he was about to arrive the word in the yard was that "the ghost walks" i.e. the boss is here! Sir Maurice's story in the museum tells of a nice twist in the tradition of the long service gold watch. Normally the employer gives it to the employee. In the wee Dumbarton museum you can see the gold watch the workers gave the boss!

The family name is still held in high regard in this Clydeside town. They were in many ways pioneering and benevolent employers; indeed one of the founders, William Denny, was way ahead of his time in the treatment of the workers, even to the extent of providing them with decent housing. This is interesting as in its declining years when the yard was thrashing around looking for work after the Second World War it even manufactured the prefab houses then seen as a short-term solution to the housing problem. The prefabs long outlasted their planned life and some were in use up to twenty years after they were built. I had an aunt in tears when it was time to move out of her beloved wee home.

Nostalgia never goes out of fashion, as the comedians say, but the real gem of the Denny Ship Tank Museum is, of course, the test tank itself. Dating from 1883 this is the oldest surviving test tank in the world. At more than 300 feet long, and still in working order, it is an impressive sight. Here designs for all sorts of hulls were tested by being dragged through calm seas and artificial waves created by paddles to test resistance, stability, speed and drag. Incidentally it was propeller tests in the tank that sparked the idea for that early helicopter mentioned. So much water was needed for the tank that it took a week to fill it though it could be emptied in a day. The model hulls themselves were created right on the site, a few feet away from the tank. All the paraphernalia of the paraffin wax moulds, carving knives and drawings are neatly displayed as if ready for use again (indeed Strathclyde University sometimes uses the tank). There is, too, a plaque in honour of engineer William Froude who was a driving force in the development of the tank. Such is the fame of the Dumbarton facility worldwide that there is a tradition that when a new tank is opened at a yard many many miles away from Dumbarton a wee bottle of water from the historic tank is added for good luck!

But the real legacy of Denny's is the ships it built, some of them the most important in maritime history. The name on everyone's lips when you talk about the famous clipper ships is *Cutty Sark*. But this, one of the most beautiful vessels to cruise the oceans of the world, is far from completely the creation of Denny's. She was indeed built at Dumbarton, in 1869, on the orders of a retired sea captain Jock Willis who sported the nickname "White Hat". There is a saying that applies, to my mind, equally to planes, cars, ships and trains – if it looks right it is right. There is no better example of this than the *Cutty Sark*. Even in dry dock, as it is now in Greenwich, it is still a truly beautiful manmade object. At sea in its heyday it must have been an awesome sight. It has been painted thousands of times and even the most mediocre of artists could not fail to catch some of its splendour. The really good portraits of it in ocean trim are unforgettable. With all sails set and pulling in a stiff breeze, it looked, even to the most prosaic of landlubbers, what it was, one of the fastest and most beautiful sailing vessels ever built. Some of the early photographs of it hint at the power its rig and its hull lines generated. One remarkable shot of it was taken by one of its skippers, Captain Richard Woodget, who took to the sea in two of the ship's boats to capture a memorable image of his command powering along far from land. This was long before "point and shoot" digital cameras with image stabilisation so to steady his primitive camera Captain Woodget lashed the ship's boats together to provide a reasonably steady platform.

Who designed this remarkable clipper? The man who takes most of the credit is Hercules Linton of shipbuilders

Scott & Linton who had a yard near the mouth of the river Leven, on land once used by William Denny & Brothers before they moved to a new site nearby. However, part of the inspiration for the *Cutty Sark* was another ship owned by Jock Willis, *The Tweed*. Willis loved the lines and speed of this ship. *The Tweed* had been built in Bombay for the East India Company and its design had been based on an old French frigate. Linton had been taken to have a look at *The Tweed* when in dry dock. Ship-owner Willis felt that much of the *The Tweed*'s speed was down to its hull lines. But Linton, although his *Cutty Sark* was to share some aspects of *The Tweed*'s design, made significant alterations including a new stern that proved very effective.

It is interesting that *The Tweed* had a figurehead of Burns' Tam o' Shanter. *Cutty Sark* followed this homage to the Ayrshire poet both in its figurehead and its actual name. Willis must have been a great Burns fan for the name *Cutty Sark* was controversial at the time since many a dour Presbyterian would be offended by the representation of a bare-breasted witch in scanty undergarments (a cutty sark) who clutched at the tail of Tam o' Shanter's mare in the great poem. The figurehead was carved by Robert Hellyer who had originally intended to have other scantily-clad witches following the figurehead along the bow. Willis, who was obviously something of a character, however, drew the line at this and he removed any further maritime erotica on the grounds of "good taste". His ego, however, allowed him to have a motto "Where there is a Willis away" inscribed along the taffrail (the rail around the ship's stern).

But it was a way not without problems. Willis wanted nothing but the best materials: East India teak above the water line, American rock elm for the bottom timbers secured by brass bolts. Other expensive techniques were used for the iron frame and the hull covering. It all cost money. Scott & Linton, formed in May 1868, signed the contract to build the *Cutty Sark* in 1869. But there had been too much optimism in the pricing of what was in effect an experimental design, with clauses specifying expensive materials and time penalties. The ship was to be built to Lloyd's A1 standard and Captain George Moodie, who was to skipper her on completion, supervised the build. Lloyd's inspectors demanded additional strengthening which burst the budget.

Scott & Linton ran out of money and instead of liquidation a deal was made for Denny's to finish the job and *Cutty Sark* was eventually launched in November 1869, by Captain Moodie's wife. But the cash problems were far from over – she was taken to Denny's own yard for the masts to be fitted (raked further aft than usual in the style of *The Tweed*) and later to Greenock for the running rigging to be installed. This caused even more money problems with the creditors.

It had been a hard fight to get *Cutty Sark* out on to the broad oceans to earn a living. But her performance, from China (the tea trade) and Australia (the wool trade) to Britain, gave birth to a true legend of the seas. Jock Willis had a long connection with the tea trade and had commanded ships owned by his father. For a spell American vessels were the fastest in this trade, but in 1868 the *Thermopylae*, built in Aberdeen, began to make voyages that marked her down as the fastest clipper on the seas. Willis built *Cutty Sark* to take her on. The race to bring tea from China to Europe was at the time followed by the press and public in a manner reminiscent of the Grand National horse race or the Derby today and, like these races, huge sums were gambled as punters backed the chances of their favourite clippers. News of how the race to England was going was telegraphed home from distant vantage points on the route.

The tea races ensured the *Cutty Sark's* reputation as one of the fastest vessels afloat and the natural assumption followed that this most beautiful of ships was a winner in the annual dash to bring home the tea. It was myth rather than fact as she never won a tea race though her massive spread of canvas and sporty lines meant she was for a time arguably the fastest vessel on the world's oceans. The most remembered tea race in 1872 saw her in a showdown with the *Thermopylae* and indeed the two famous clippers battled neck and neck for hundreds of miles, though the *Cutty Sark* lost her rudder for a time in heavy seas in the Indian Ocean and the delay meant she arrived seven days later than her rival. But, as in horse racing, the gamblers could still speculate but for that piece of bad luck she would have won. If only . . .

It was all part of the last hurrah for the windjammers. The Suez Canal had just opened and now the steamers which were beginning to conquer the freight routes had a short cut to the Far East. By the end of the decade the *Cutty Sark* had left the tea trade and, in a sad comedown, now carried a more prosaic cargo – coal. Her appearance and her reputation both took a hammering in the early 1880s. There was even a murder and a suicide on board her and a minor mutiny. But that remarkable man Jock Willis was not finished yet and he spied an opportunity presented by the Australian wool trade. Once again her legendary speed made headlines and there were record voyages between Melbourne, Sydney and London. In these new glory days the skipper was the eccentric Richard Woodget, mentioned earlier. But by 1895 beauty and speed was not enough to keep her on top in a changing maritime environment. A career back in Britain as a training ship beckoned, but before that reasonably dignified end to her ocean voyaging there were a few years under Portuguese ownership with all sorts of cargoes from Europe to Africa and the Americas. The glories of the tea races were history now.

She was saved from the ultimate humiliation of the breaker's yard by an old clipper hand, a Captain Dowman, who bought her and opened her to the public in Falmouth. On his death she was used as a training ship for Royal Navy and merchant navy cadets before she was replaced by a newer and more suitable vessel. In 1951, the Cutty Sark Society was formed by admirers and cash was raised to get her a permanent place in dry dock in Greenwich.

This presented a new danger rather than ocean storms – fire. The ship required massive repair work to get her back into good condition after years of neglect to ensure her long-term survival. Such work is always tricky, especially in a wooden ship, and a major fire, linked to the renovation, in 2007 did much damage. And there was another fire in 2014 though it was less severe. The cost of renovation was already horrendous and these fires added millions to the bill. The money, however, was found and today the *Cutty Sark* is still a major tourist attraction. Preserving the memory of a great sailing ship is a victory even more valuable than winning a tea race!

3

Aircraft, Hovercraft and the Famous Irrawaddy Flotilla

If the story of the *Cutty Sark* is the headline maker of the early history of Denny's, what followed is no less intriguing though not quite as glamorous. The end of the windjammer era removed perhaps the most glorious sight to be seen on the seas: a tall four-master all sails set and creaming along in a good breeze at speeds as high as 18 knots. Though the designers and builders of these ocean "greyhounds" had an eye for beauty and form they also realised the money-making opportunities of the advent of steam and other methods of mechanical propulsion. Denny's is a classic example of a yard that could adapt and innovate to keep the cash flow strong. Even in its dying days the yard was game for change and turned to building aircraft and hover-craft as the shipbuilding market changed worldwide.

But many years before the sound of the wrecker's ball was echoing around douce Dumbarton, in the shadow of the famous rock and castle, the yard had other ploys that added to maritime history and helped cement the reputation of ships built on the Clyde. One of the most remarkable, and largely now forgotten, was the creation of what became known as the Irrawaddy Flotilla. No vessels could be more removed from the beauty of the clippers than these unspectacular river ferries built mostly by Denny's though other Clyde yards like Yarrow's, A. & J. Inglis and Robert Duncan & Company of Port Glasgow also built vessels for use on the Irrawaddy – by far the most important trade route in Burma which still has a poor transport infrastructure. The Irrawaddy is one of the great rivers of the world, flowing from the Himalayas to the Bay of Bengal. In places it is up to four miles wide. Often dangerously shallow and tortuous, particularly in the delta, it is affected by the melting snows on high mountain peaks far inland and regular monsoons which mean its width and depth both fluctuate remarkably. This posed problems for the designers of the ferries that plied this mighty waterway. The need for shallow draft meant that paddle power was important and that the hull and upper works had to be particularly strong. Mostly the ferries were around 200 feet long though later models were up to 300 feet. Denny's in particular had the expertise and also built river ferries for use on the Ganges, the Nile and even the Mississippi (among them the legendary *Delta Queen*).

The Scottish connection in Rangoon was strong. From the 1860s to the 1940s the ferries were run by the Irrawaddy Flotilla Company, known as the IFC, which had at one time around 11,000 staff – engineers, crew, administrators and sundry others. The company behind it was the famous Paddy Henderson shipping line of Glasgow and, until Burma gained independence in 1948, most of the British employees were Scots. At its peak the company operated around 500 vessels, a combination of paddle steamers and barges. An impressive flotilla indeed. A large number of the ships in the fleet were Clyde built. Denny's built three of the most impressive and the fastest – the *Japan*, *Mysore* and *Siam*.

A man who knows more than most about this unique operation is the noted historian Tim Willasey-Wilsey, a former senior research fellow of King's College London and one-time director of the Foreign and Commonwealth Office, a much travelled man. In an account of a trip to Burma a few years ago he quotes an IFC document of the thirties which described the diversity of cargo carried by the flotilla: "Great bales of cotton, bags of rice, blocks of jade, lacquer ware, silk, tamarind, elephants sometimes, woven mats, maize, jaggery, bullocks, marble Buddhas, oil cake, tobacco, timber." In upward-bound cargoes would be found all the various imports from Europe: motor cars, corrugated iron, condensed milk, matches, aluminium-ware, sewing machines, piece goods, soap, cigarettes, cement and whisky. Of his trip he writes: "If you take the Irrawaddy River route from the ancient temples of Bagan to the second city of Mandalay you will see, moored to the bank, a large old paddle steamer that used to belong to the Irrawaddy Flotilla Company. It is the *Minthamee* ordered in 1948 from Yarrow's of Scotstoun. Renamed the *Moiat Yadana* it was commandeered by the late dictator General Ne Win, who ruled Burma from 1962 until 1988, and used as his private yacht and later as a restaurant. It is now the last surviving paddle steamer on the Irrawaddy." The Second World War saw the end of the great days for the flotilla. The fear was that this important transport asset would fall into the hands of the Japanese and to prevent this, 200 vessels were sunk at Mandalay and others scuppered at Katha.

When Burma became independent in 1948 the flotilla was nationalised and some new orders were placed with Yarrow's and Denny's to build up the fleet along with any salvaged vessels. These days, looking at any rusting and patched-up remnants of the Clyde ships on the Irrawaddy, the question the layman is most likely to ask is: how did they get to the river? The answer was in packing cases. The Clyde yards completed the ships in Scotland then developed the technique of "knock down" and the various parts shipped by ocean-going freighters were reassembled at their destinations. The IFC had its own shipyard in Rangoon for this purpose.

If the vessels of the Irrawaddy flotilla lacked glamour, another of the "knock down" specials was quite the opposite. It became perhaps the best known river transport in the world. When the parts shipped from Dumbarton were assembled in America the *Delta Queen* was a handsome sight – the epitome of the stern wheeled riverboats that plied the Mississippi and featured in countless Hollywood epics. Tall funnels spewing out thick black smoke, the sound of a riverboat steam organ (calliope) drifting across the delta, the sight of high-rolling gamblers, glass in hand and resplendent in fancy waistcoats and decks where beautiful women promenaded in their crinolines made for good box office for many years. The very name *Delta Queen* to this day conjures up mental flashbacks of such stars as James Garner.

4

Triumph, Tragedy and Up the Clyde on a Banana Boat

Across the river from Dumbarton, as the Clyde widens on its lengthy journey to the sea down from the centre of Glasgow, lie the remains of what was once, perhaps, the most numerous collections of large shipyards in the world dotted one after another on a few miles of riverside. Greenock and Port Glasgow lived and breathed ship-building with hardly a resident not connected in one way or another with the industry. The variety of yards, large and small, was such that you could not accurately describe the area as a company town, but that was the ethos. Greenock and Port Glasgow had many of the characteristics of such a place, particularly the aforementioned interlocking financial dependency of those who lived and did business there even if they did not work directly in the yards.

To get the flavour of the place in the time before the decline I talked to Professor Tom Bone who grew up in Port Glasgow where the yards provided the only major industry from the early 1820s until about 1955 or so. (The one other major industrial concern was the curiously named Gourock Ropeworks – its base was in Port Glasgow! – which had been created to serve mainly local shipbuilding, though it diversified in its later years.) Tom, a former Principal of Jordanhill College and Deputy Principal of Strathclyde University, was a leading figure in Scottish education in the 1970s, 80s and early 90s. His academic success marked him out from many of his school friends who were content to aspire to a job in the yards. His background though was fairly typical. His father's father had been a manager in the Ropeworks, and his father in his early years worked in the yards. His mother's father worked as a caulker in the shipyards for more than fifty years, managing to survive the depression of the 1920s and 30s because his wife, Tom's grandmother, had a little shop in the bay area of the town. Tom told me that he thought his grandfather had worked at one time on the *Glenlee*, now immaculately restored and moored upriver at the Museum of Transport and enjoying a new life as an eye-catching tourist attraction known as Glasgow's "Tall Ship".

Another member of the family, his mother's brother Bill, had a career similar to many other young men of the area. He left his yard job at sixteen and went off to the First World War. On his return, jobs in the yards were hard to come by. He took the boat across the pond and found work in America. His younger brother Paul, too young to fight in the trenches, got employment in the yards in the late 1920s. He was so successful he, too, left the Port but only for the short journey to the other side of Scotland where he went on to be general manager of Henry Robb's Shipyard in Leith. You can take the boy out of the Port as they say, but you can't take the shipbuilding out of the boy! Tom grew up during the Second World War when Greenock and Port Glasgow were targets for German bombers and many lives were lost, though not on the scale of the Clydebank blitz on the north side of the river.

The drone of enemy bombers and shrieks of the air raid sirens were familiar sounds at the time. But the saddest memory Tom Bone has of his schooldays was the loss of four friends who died, not at the hands of the German bombers. These lads were killed in a horrific incident on the local railway line. They were attempting to gather packets of chewing gum thrown from a train by American sailors going up to Glasgow for a spot of rest and recreation and were hit by a train going in the opposite direction. You never forget something like that. When it came time to leave school there was again plenty of work in the yards and most of Tom's friends had shipyard connections of one kind or other. He told me: "To a boy growing up it seemed that shipbuilding was an activity that would always be there." And when he went to university, the first of his family to do so, the prospects for Port Glasgow seemed brighter than they turned out to be. But, now in his eighties Tom still thinks well of the "wee Port".

These days when there is talk of the lower Clyde yards the names that spring to mind are generally Scotts (builders of the Clyde's first Dreadnought and the first submarine), Lithgow's or Ferguson. Researching Scotts it was clear that it had a high reputation in general as a submarine builder. But in its story there was a flavour of one of the seeds that led eventually, along with industrial troubles and foreign competition, to the decline of the Clyde in the sixties and seventies. Dan Conley, a Campbeltown man who rose to the command of a nuclear sub, recalled a visit to the yard in his early days as a submariner when the overall impression was of a place past its best, a facility that had not kept up with changing times. Mind you, Commander Conley was even more scathing at working practices in the navy's own shipyard at Portsmouth at the time. In a highly readable autobiography he noted that doing a night shift meant a couple of hours' work before midnight then five or six hours of kip out of sight of any bosses! Shipyards were not alone in this abuse – living near the old Rolls Royce aero engine factory in East Kilbride I was aware of locals who ran thriving businesses by day and slept the night away in the factory. It is said that some even had their own bed. Commander Conley was also critical of visits to Yarrow's when working on navy procurement, when he saw special coatings being applied to warship decking under the insufficient shelter of poly sheets to keep off the wind and rain. Such work in up-to-date yards should, he thought, have been done indoors. Yarrow's, however, did modernise later and became a continually respected builder of warships. But Commander Conley – who was to become a major figure in the history of the sub base at Faslane – provided strong evidence that all was not as it should have been at the time of that particular visit.

But there are scores more shipbuilders in the area that have drifted out of the memory of most. Yards like William Simons & Co., Steele and Co., John Wood, William Hamilton, Caird & Co. and William Russell. And many more. But if the names of the owners are sometimes forgotten, many of the memories of working in the yards are still told. One man who remembers the good times well, in yards on both sides of the river, is Scott Whiteford who is a retired naval architect who started his career in Scott Lithgow's Ltd. in the early seventies and finished at BAE Systems, Scotstoun, (formerly Yarrow Shipbuilders Ltd.), having worked as senior manager on many commercial and naval ship design projects, including the latest Queen Elizabeth Class aircraft carriers.

Scott was a good man to talk to about working conditions in the yards but first, in less serious vein, he had some humorous tales to tell. A favourite was from the time he was working as a young graduate at Scotts' Cartsburn yard in Greenock. He told me: "I worked alongside an older draughtsman/designer by the name of Alec Aitken. He told me that when he was a draughtsman during the Second World War he was sent out to a merchant ship off Greenock to measure her up for some modifications that had to be done at a later date. He was deep in the bowels of the ship taking notes and making measurements. He heard a lot of noise on deck, but thought nothing of it as the crew could have been testing some of the ship's machinery. He carried on and completed his notes and sketches. When he eventually returned on deck he noticed that they were heading out towards the open Atlantic, past the anti-submarine boom that stretched from the Gourock to Dunoon during the Second World War. He asked a crew member where they were heading and back came the reply – Murmansk!

"Alec was in sports jacket, collar and tie as all draughtsmen dressed in these days, and his wife was expecting him home for tea that evening. He then recounted some amusing adventures when the ship dropped him off at Scapa Flow. He had the devil of a journey back to Greenock with no identification papers, no money and a very weak tale to tell the military police. He eventually got home some days later. The same Alec was a victim of a joke by his work-mates. He brought his golf clubs to work in preparation for an outing later in the day. Unbeknown to him some of the other draughtsmen hid two lead weights in the bottom of his golf bag. He finished his round more than usually exhausted and only then did the jokers let him into their secret. Humour was not in short supply in Scotts and another memory was building a drill ship called the *Ben Ocean Lancer*. It had what was called a 'moon pool' used for drilling purposes that was effectively open to the sea and collected a lot of debris floating in it, plastic bottles and odds and ends of ropes etc. As a ruse, one of the ship's managers called over a foreman and instructed him to pump out the moon pool so that the rubbish could be cleared away. After several hours of rigging hoses and running pumps etc. the foreman eventually came to the manager and in frustration said to him, 'I canna understand it, the water's nae going oot!'"

A classic of shipyard humour came Scott's way when working in Yarrow's in the eighties. Robert Easton, later Sir Robert, was the managing director at the time. His son Murray was on the Yarrow's Management Development scheme and trying hard to establish himself with the unenviable task of being the chairman's son. Murray was a ship manager in production and had a Portacabin as his office. The yard workers soon put a sign over his front door . . ."The House of the Rising Son". Names and forms of address were important in the yards, almost as important as that manager's badge of office – the bowler hat. When Sir Eric Yarrow was chairman of the board Scott remembers his friend Bill Thomson in the design office telling him of his occasional contacts with the great man when tenders had to be produced in haste. "I am on first name terms with Sir Eric," he told Scott. "He calls me Bill and I call him sir." Plenty of humour, but plenty of great ships, too.

Scott Whiteford is interesting, too, on the changes down the years to working hours, health and safety and other issues. He told me: "For most of my working life we did forty hours a week, then latterly thirty-seven. As a manager I did not get paid overtime, but many staff were always pleased when the yards were busy and they were offered overtime on Tuesdays and Thursdays and either time and a half on Saturday or double time on a Sunday. Yard owners always maintained a culture of clocking in and clocking out. I never much liked this as it encouraged people to stick to set hours. For many years I worked for engineering consultants Yard Ltd. where there was no clocking in, but if you were busy you worked extra hours and in quiet periods you were allowed a little leeway like leaving early on a Friday for example. That system worked better for me and most staff preferred it."

He went on: "Canteens/staff restaurants were very hierarchical. There could be one for blue-collar workers, one for junior staff, senior staff and one for directors in yards like Scott Lithgow and Yarrow's in the seventies and eighties. I remember being invited to attend the senior managers' restaurant – it felt like a major promotion. Eventually this structure tended to change into one or two canteens. Everyone at Scotts would remember "Big Minnie" who was a waitress in the Greenock canteen. She was a tyrant but loved by one and all. She got to know everyone's name and their likes so that when you were choosing from the menu she would have your first choice hidden behind her back which as you said 'steak pie' she would set down with a triumphant thump on the table!"

Scott then told me of changes in that controversial, and often wrongly maligned, matter of health and safety, which he says "has come on in leaps and bounds". A good thing, too. Yards were always dangerous places to work. Heavy sheets of metal being hoisted in and out of crowded work areas, welding going on and red hot rivets flying through the air made it vital to keep your wits about you. But serious accidents in building the great ships were inevitable. One of Scott's earliest and darkest memories was at Scotts shipyard. A foreman was standing in a machinery space, guiding the crane driver to lower a bow thrust unit into place. The lugs holding the unit gave way and it dropped on to the poor foreman below. A horrible, quick and unnecessary death.

"Fortunately, procedures in place nowadays make such fatalities much much less likely," says Scott. "We all knew of people who had worked with asbestos in the early days when the risks were not understood who later died from the effects of close contact to such a hazardous material. The importance of safety now comes from the very top of the management organisations and all staff are advised that they are each personally responsible and that they should raise safety concerns immediately with a line manager."

These anecdotes give a flavour of working life that applies to all the Clyde yards, not just Scott Lithgow's. But behind the simple one-word name Lithgow known to everyone on Clydeside lies a fascinatingly complex tale of success and ambition largely fuelled by the Lithgow family. It resulted at one stage in more or less complete domination of shipbuilding in the towns of Port Glasgow and Greenock. Unlike Brown's and Fairfield upriver, Lithgow's did not build flashy liners like the great Cunarders or the beautiful White Empress fleet. Gilded ballrooms, swimming pools, luxurious restaurants and saloons, well stocked with the finest champagne and brandy, were not part of the recipe – the domination was created by relentlessly producing well-designed hard-working commercial vessels year after year, ore carriers and oil tankers in particular. In both world wars the number of ships built was awesome. Between 1914 and 1918 the output was jaw-dropping though only one vessel was for the Royal Navy, a fast patrol boat called *P21*. This was eclipsed in the Second World War when Lithgow-owned yards produced ninety-seven ships totalling almost a million and a half tons. The bulk of this output was made up of thirty-three tramps of the Empire design, but small aircraft carriers, fifty-four merchant ships for private owners, and transport ferries also glided down the slipways to splash noisily into the brown waters of the

Clyde. After the war the yards made a name for well-built tankers with an occasional cargo liner thrown in. Incidently during the seventies and eighties Scott Lithgow also produced container ships, research vessels, super tankers (up to 500,000 tonnes) and dynamic positioned drillships. They also built large semi-submersibles for the offshore oil industry before eventual closure.

One category of ship still, occasionally, features in the pub chat of the older generations, reviewing life through a pint glass. Clydesiders are generally regarded as street smart and witty with a ready humorous response to any query. Years ago, a favourite retort when asked a question with an obvious answer would often be: "Do you think I came up the Clyde in a banana boat?" (i.e. Do you think I am stupid?) These days it might seem an obscure observation, but in the thirties, banana boats were a commonplace sight on the river. Four of the most famous were built in Port Glasgow: *Jamaica Pioneer, Jamaica Progress, Jamaica Producer* and *Jamaica Planter*. These ships were owned by a London company formed to carry passengers and cargo on outbound voyages to the West Indies and bananas back to Europe. Only *Producer* was to have a normal service life. The Germans sank *Pioneer* and *Progress* within four weeks of each other in 1940 and *Planter* was sunk in a collision in Barry Roads towards the end of the war.

The early photographs of launches at Port Glasgow show other river legends in action – the "Flying" fleet of tugs. The Clyde Shipping Company with a history dating back to the early 1800s had a tradition of preceding the name of their vessels with the word "Flying" as in *Flying Scout, Flying Foam* etc. In the story of the Clyde the tugs of the Clyde Shipping Company and other companies play a major role, on hand at launches and at all hours and in all weathers assisting vessels to berth in often difficult to get to quaysides and alongside cranes. Theirs is a story of generally unspectacular hard daily grind on the river. Some say even the word "tug" has its roots in the river, "tug" used instead of "dragging". It is sad to record that the *Flying Phantom,* the last tug built on the Clyde for service on the Clyde tragically cost three lives when in 2007 it was accidentally sunk off Clydebank.

5

Supertankers, a Super Salesman and Blue-Sky Thinking

Sophisticated refrigerated fruit carriers, super tankers and enormously powerful tugs were all a long way into the future. The story started around 1874 when the company which, despite many changes of name down the years, was to become known simply as Lithgow's was established after Joseph Russell and his partners, Anderson Rodger and William Lithgow, leased the Bay Yard in Port Glasgow from one of the earliest Clyde shipbuilders Cunliffe & Dunlop. They started trading as Russell & Company and among the most notable vessels they built was the beautiful *Falls of Clyde*, a three-masted barque whose chequered history is dealt with in detail later in this book. A year after the launch of this historic vessel the three partners bought the Cartsdyke Mid Yard from J.E. Scott and a couple years later the Kingston yard from Henry Murray. The march to domination was picking up speed. In 1891 the original partnership was dissolved when Russell retired. Anderson Rodger took the Bay Yard and Lithgow the Kingston and Cartsdyke yards. In 1900 the Cartsdyke yard was sold to

Greenock Dockyard and a further eight years on William Lithgow's sons James and Henry assumed control of the company.

The history books make much of Henry Ford and his standardisation and conveyer belt techniques in car building. But it is fascinating to note that more than a hundred years ago the benefits of such ideas were recognised in Clyde yards. Russell's, for example, were said to have produced around fifty sailing ships based on a single hull mould. In the early days only sailing ships were built in the Kingston yard and standard tramp steamers at the Bay and Greenock yards. The early builders were innovative in money matters as well – they took a financial interest in some of the vessels they had built and sold. Other vessels built "on spec" were traded by the partners themselves if they were not sold. The adoption of such innovative engineering and financial techniques in the early years sparked spectacular growth.

Shipbuilding in Port Glasgow took a further spurt in 1908 when William Lithgow's sons James and Henry took control and the expansion of the empire continued with the acquisition of the East Yard from Robert Duncan & Co. in 1915. In 1918 Russell & Company was renamed Lithgow's Ltd. For the next twenty years there was almost an acquisition a year and by the early 1920s the brothers owned all the yards in Port Glasgow. One of the many acquisitions, Robert Duncan & Company, was responsible for a vessel still remembered for its remarkable beauty and style, particularly in Campbeltown and Carradale in Argyll – the SS Dalriada. It was launched in 1926 for the Campbeltown and Glasgow Steam Packet Company and for years it was an invaluable connection between remote Kintyre and the city of Glasgow and the towns around it. Some call Kintyre the "mainland island" because in the north it is only a mile or so wide, the land gap between East and West Loch Tarbet so short that when the Vikings roamed the west coast one of their leaders known as Magnus Bare Legs dragged his ships the short distance from one sea loch to the other down what is now the A83. Even today access to the villages and hamlets dotted around Kintyre is difficult, with access via the Rest and Be Thankful (a mountain pass with a steep and winding road to its summit on the way to Inveraray and the west coast) frequently blocked by landslides or single-track roads blocked by car accidents. The *Dalriada* was a lifeline for passengers and cargo. While it is remembered for that valuable trade link, when people talk about it they tend to mention her beauty. She had the style of what we would call today a super yacht, rather than being mere commercial transportation. Seldom have beauty and capability been so effectively combined. Sadly the *Dalriada* came to a desperate end. In 1941 it was requisitioned by the Admiralty and less than a year later it sank after hitting a mine while helping to clear a wreck in the Thames estuary.

After the Second World War, Lithgow's branched out in another direction earning a reputation as a world leader in building supertankers. In the early part of the seventies the vessel that made the headlines was the *Nordic Clansman* which weighed in at just over 100,000 tons. This was an enormous size of a vessel, even on the Clyde, but it was soon to be surpassed as a giant of the ocean, by a tanker called *World Score* which could almost be called two ships. The vessel had been launched in 1974 as the *Cartsdyke Glen*, a name based on the two main yards of Scott Lithgow at the time. The fore and aft sections of this immense ship, 126,000 tons, were built separately and were joined afloat in 1978 and she went into service as the *World Score* for the Niarchos Group. She sailed for twelve years under this flag before being renamed *Kosmos Sailor*. She then joined the

Bergesen fleet as *Berge Forrest* for nine years. Her end came in 2002 when in another name change she was the *Ancona*. Her building had been a glorious spectacular on the Clyde. For years the two huge halves, and finally the finished giant, dominated the riverside at Port Glasgow, towering over the motorway and nearby Glasgow–Gourock railway line and making passing cars, lorries and trains look like toys.

Her final days were less glorious – scrapped on the infamous beach at Chittagong, torn apart by hundreds of workers swarming over her using primitive tools to winkle out every usable piece of steel regardless of risk. If in her days in Port Glasgow and sailing the world's oceans she had been an uplifting and awesome sight, her end was a depressing affair, all dignity gone, beached for the entire world like some dead sea monster, any respect for her place in maritime history seeping into oily sand. The infamous Chittagong yard started back in 1960 when a cyclone left one vessel stranded on the sand for years. Eventually a company on the hunt for steel bought her and an industry was born. *World Score* was not alone as a pitiful sight. The breaking "yards" on this coastal strip of Bangladesh were at one time the largest such enterprise in the world. Working on the beach on the crumbling skeletons of once great ships was dangerous. It is a sad commentary on human nature that for a spell the place was even a malign tourist attraction with people watching low-paid workers, without financial security, protective clothing or modern equipment toiling on the beaches. Outsiders are no longer welcome on these beaches and little wonder – a local watchdog group claimed that on average one worker a week died in an accident. Magazines, newspapers and TV documentaries world-wide exposed the exploitation that was going on and the publicity had some effect. The global shipping company

Maersk stopped using the beaches as a place to scrap its unwanted ships. This decision was followed in 2014 by Hapag-Lloyd despite the fact that the cost of scrapping was higher elsewhere.

The success of building ships in vast sections and joining them together elsewhere is now commonplace and is being currently used in the construction of the new Queen Elizabeth class of aircraft carriers for the Royal Navy. Back in the seventies it was what some like to call "blue-sky thinking". And the man responsible for the thinking was one of the most remarkable men to work in shipbuilding on the Clyde, Sir Ross Belch. In a perceptive obituary in *The Herald* in 1999 full acknowledgement was made to his contribution to shipbuilding both as a technical innovator and for his work in the fraught area of worker-management relations. The backstory of the *World Score* is interesting. Shipbuilding is a roller coaster of an industry, a mixture of periods when multi-million pound orders fly in through open windows and periods when salesmen have to tour the world in search of orders. It was during one of the downturns that Ross Belch came into his own, securing vital orders against the odds.

The sort of operator he was is demonstrated by the fact that when in the Far East he took million-pound orders for the yard, ignoring the rather significant detail that the wanted ships were seemingly too big to be built in Port Glasgow. Back in Scotland there was much head-scratching by the technical teams before the revolutionary idea of building two separate halves and joining the pieces when afloat came about. It was a master stroke and the first time this had been done in tidal waters. Scott Whiteford told me "I remember this well". They aligned the hulls using lasers on the upper deck, constructed a "cofferdam" around the connection of the two hulls, pumped out the water and thereby allowed welders in to complete the final welds. To build the cofferdam they brought an old retired plater out of retirement especially. The first time they pumped out the water they caught a salmon in the cofferdam!

Belch was something of a polymath and his spectacular achievements in the world of shipbuilding technology tended to steal the headlines from other valuable work. The point was underlined in his *Herald* obituary which opined that: "He came to prominence in the industry shortly after the Second World War and for the next forty years he was never far from the heart of things as a Clyde shipbuilder and a powerful defender of British shipbuilding interests. On Clydeside, where he started his career as an apprentice in the Fairfield yard at Govan, he became known as an innovator both of shipbuilding methods and in industrial relations. As managing director first of Lithgow's in Port Glasgow and later of the Scott Lithgow group in Greenock, he arguably did more than anyone in the industry to transform worker-management relations."

This remarkable man was as at home in the noise and bustle of dusty fabrication yards as he was round an elegant boardroom table or out on the road searching for orders. He was a super salesman and his successes in this field were remarkable for he was operating at a time when the industry was struggling against competition from the Far East and eastern Europe. That skill in negotiating served him well when as president of the Shipbuilders and Repairers National Association he led the industry in talks with the government to set up nationalisation in 1976. Later he was a leading member of a committee set up to decide the shape of the industry in the new regime. During this period he joined the board of British Shipbuilders, retiring in 1979. That achievement was no surprise to followers of his career. He was marked out for the top from the day he first went through the gates of Fairfield's as a youngster.

He was a medallist when at Morrison's Academy in Crieff, won first-class honours in naval architecture at the University of Glasgow and was director and general manager at Lithgow's aged thirty-four. It was rocket-like progress in an industry where experience was worshipped. But the founding fathers of shipbuilding on the Clyde, a hundred or so years before Ross Belch, were often energetic and intelligent young men with the ability to innovate rather than rely on trusted formulas. Shipbuilding must have been as the cliché has it "in his blood" even if Ross Belch was born in London. His father was a Glasgow solicitor who had gone south to work for the Shipbuilding Employers Federation. But Belch senior had the belief, common enough then and now, that in matters of education Scotland was supreme and hence the young Ross was schooled in rural Perthshire, a far cry from the tenements of Port Glasgow and Greenock or foggy old London. But thoughts of shipbuilding were never far away whether in London or Crieff and it is significant that the youngster's first visit to a Clyde yard was to John Brown's in Clydebank for the 1934 launch of the *Queen Mary* – construction had begun on the ship in 1930 when the vessel was known simply as Hull 534 in the yard and the town.

Ross Belch was a giant of the Clyde just as much as the famous ships he built. His energy and work rate are still remembered by the older generation. They still talk of the "Sunday Club". A day of rest for most, he used the time to convene meetings with executives from the Lower Clyde yards to discuss progress and problems with ongoing projects. Those of us who love the lore of the Clyde have a lot to thank him for – he had a major role in setting up the Scottish Maritime Museum in Irvine. It is also fitting to note that one of his proudest achievements was in retaining Ferguson's yard in Port Glasgow in the early 1990s. However this specialist yard was to face a commercial rocky road in the years ahead before a renaissance and renewed hope in the new century. More of this in the final chapter of this book.

But latterly the story of the lower Clyde was one of decline.

6

The Legendary Waverley and Other Icons

Regeneration of docklands round the world is a multi-million pound game with pinstripe property developers in glossy offices reeling in massive profits from areas which in past days were the domain, not of paper shuffling office workers, but of hard-working men and women who toiled long hours till the sweat dripped, using muscle as well as brain. London, Melbourne and, yes, Glasgow, now boast dockland residential skyscrapers, science centres, and theatres, some of which look like they have escaped from some futuristic comic-book storyline. In Glasgow there is a delicious irony in that right beside the glass-walled science centre itself there sits on the river one of the most significant and beautiful vessels ever to claim the title Clydebuilt – the *Waverley*, said to be the last seagoing paddle steamer in the world. In the summer season its eye-catching bright red and black funnels add a splash of colour amid concrete and glass. The owners of the high flats on the riverside on summer days take to their balconies to wave to the tourists on the old paddler. It is an icon from another era. Daily it sets off downriver on a series of mini cruises that show the Firth of Clyde at its best and the Clyde itself as a place dramatically different from its heyday. Shopping centres replace once bustling shipyards. There is a plethora of new housing and green spaces. Normally at its base in the city centre the *Waverley* is moored with its bow upstream. Turning it to face the sea is a daily ritual much enjoyed by the passengers themselves, who form large queues to board long before the time comes to cast off.

The *Waverley* is of shallow draught designed to let it roam the sea lochs of the west coast and take on and disembark passengers from the many famous Clyde piers like Dunoon, Rothesay and Largs. But it is not as nimble as a propeller vessel, no bow and stern thrusters here, just those huge wooden paddles pushed around by 2,100 horse power triple expansion reciprocating engines with the steam provided by oil-fired boilers. Incidentally it might be worth digressing a little to point out here that the engines are in an area open to the public and are a magnificent sight as the engineers scan dials and pull levers to respond to the ringing of the telegraph from the bridge. If you ever get the chance of a wee sail on the *Waverley* make sure you are in the engine room area when she takes a pier. To digress a little further, looking at the engines is worthwhile in more ways than one. When I was a youngster sailing the firth with my family, if my dad was temporarily missing I was always told he was "looking at the engines" – this was code for nipping down below for a swift pint and was a ruse much used by drouthy male holidaying Glaswegians of the day.

Back to the departure routine! The design might have been fine for the firth but it presents problems going about in the narrow confines upriver. When moored facing upriver it often needed a tug to pull the bow out into the current which was strong enough to nudge the whole ship slowly round to face downstream. These days a powerful RIB (Rigid Inflatable Boat) uses massive outboards to give the necessary heave to turn the bow into the current, but it is still worth watching. Now, slowly gathering speed as the *Waverley* heads for the Tail of the Bank and the open firth, the first few hundred yards or so provide a first-class view of another river icon – the three-masted barque *Glenlee*. This is what Glaswegians call the "tall ship" and it has been immaculately restored and moored outside the Glasgow Riverside Museum (opened in 2011). The *Glenlee* is a classic story of restoration. It was one of a small class of steel hulled bulk carriers built for a city firm, Alexander Sterling & Co. Worked hard, it plied the oceans from its launch in the 1880s at the now largely forgotten Bay Yard in Port Glasgow until the 1920s when it was bought by the Spanish Navy for use as a sail training vessel. In its commercial life it circumnavigated the globe several times and rounded the dreaded Cape Horn no less than fifteen times. It is one of only five Clydebuilt sailing ships afloat worldwide, and all are tourist attractions. I have been on board two of the most famous, the *Balclutha* in San Francisco and the *Falls of Clyde* now facing an uncertain future in Honolulu and in poor condition. I can vouch for the quality of restoration of the *Glenlee* at first hand, it is simply superb. Incidentally the complex work of restoring the rigging used the expertise of some experienced hands from San Francisco's maritime museum.

The *Glenlee* is almost unrecognisable from the rusting hulk that lay forgotten in Seville harbour in 1981 before it was bought by the Clyde Maritime Trust for around £40,000. The initial cost was the least of it and future generations visiting the ship will appreciate the financial assistance that went into preserving such a valuable piece of maritime history. Apart from the Trust, money came from European funds, lottery cash, Glasgow City Council and private donations. It is moored in front of the Riverside Museum. In certain light conditions the reflection of the ship on the walls of the museum is striking. The Riverside Museum was designed by the late internationally renowned Zaha Hadid, an Iraqi-British architect who in 2004 became the first woman recipient of the Pritzker Architecture Prize and received the Stirling Prize in 2010 and 2011.

The Riverside exterior lives up to the hype with an amazing roofline of huge zigzags of metal and a glass frontage that brilliantly reflects the graceful lines of the *Glenlee*. It won the title of European Museum of the Year in 2013 and is now established as a major Scottish tourist attraction though the interior – not the work of Ms Hadid – is, to my mind, overstuffed with exhibits and some frankly daft decisions like displaying cars up the face of a wall inaccessible to enthusiasts. Still worth a visit, especially when there is the chance to see artworks normally on show in the Imperial War Museum in London, in particular, the paintings of Sir Stanley Spencer who died in 1959. Most art lovers best remember him for so-called "biblical paintings" set in the picturesque Thames-side village of Cookham and his controversial nudes. But Spencer had a remarkable connection with the very different Clyde. During the Second World War, he was commissioned by the War Artists' Advisory Committee. Spencer's agent wrote to the committee asking for employment and they agreed to send him to Lithgow's Port Glasgow shipyard in 1940. He was tasked with producing eleven canvases, some up to six metres long. The first two, "burners" and "caulkers", were finished by the end of his first summer in Scotland and the War Artists' Advisory Committee paid £300, not a princely sum even in those far off days, for them.

The artistic and eccentric artist Spencer must have at

times seemed a fish out of water amid the grimy hard workers who lived in the tenements of Port Glasgow. But strangely he got on well with local folk and his paintings brilliantly caught the wartime spirit of the Clydesiders. The art establishment may have admired the paintings, but the then owner of the yard, James Lithgow, disagreed and indeed complained about the way it was portrayed to the War Artists' Advisory Committee. Spencer stayed around Clydeside on and off for years and was still painting in 1944. After the war ended the advisory committee offered the Clyde series of paintings to the National Maritime Museum, their seemingly natural home, but they ended up in the War Museum. When in 2006 the paintings needed some restoration work the museum asked football legend Sir Alex Ferguson to use his Clydeside connections to help with the project. A good move since "Fergie's" father, brother and uncle had worked in the yards when Spencer was in Scotland. The restoration complete, the War Museum agreed to send some of the paintings north for loan periods to the Riverside Museum.

If the inside of the Riverside arouses different opinions, there is, the *Glenlee* apart, a series of outdoor exhibits definitely worth a visit. Here you can watch the progress of restoration under way at the point where the Kelvin flows into the Clyde. Of particular note is the restoration of one of the small pedestrian ferries – Number 8 – which used to cross the Clyde in the days before the Kingston Bridge, the "Squinty" bridge, or the Glasgow Arc to give it its Sunday name, and footbridges took away its trade.

This space was the yard of A. & J. Inglis, builders of the *Waverley* itself no less, and the iconic Loch Lomond vessel *Maid of the Loch* which is now being restored for the umpteenth time after years lying semi-derelict at Balloch.

41

7

A Short Bus Ride into History and Death Under the Waves

Growing up in Glasgow in the forties and fifties, it was almost impossible not to be aware of the great shipyards of the Clyde, though most of them were at some distance from the city centre itself. The maritime heritage of the place came alive in travel agents' windows with their highly coloured and evocative posters of the great transatlantic liners and the beginnings of today's massive cruising industry. The impact of the shipbuilding industry was also heard in the pub talk of the many thousands who, still in their grimy working clothes and drouthy after a day of hard physical labour, stopped for a pint or three on their way home. The newspapers of these days, before television and radio took over as the prime source of news, were filled with reports of the comings and goings on the river and the progress on the latest world-class vessels under construction in the yards. At one time the city boasted in addition to a lively morning paper scene no less than three evening papers – the *Evening Times,* the *Evening News* and the *Evening Citizen* – and the centre of town resounded to a familiar cry in the early afternoon as the street-corner vendors plied their wares: *"Times, News* and *Cit-i-zen."* All three covered the waterfront, as Hollywood would say, in great detail. My own interest in shipbuilding was sparked by my father reading out the words hammered out on aged typewriters by the various newspaper shipping correspondents from his armchair with a glass of something stimulating at hand. And short trips to see one yard in particular at close quarters, Fairfield's of Govan, the nearest to the city centre. We lived in the south side suburb of Croftfoot and from there ran the 4A Corporation bus which took you on a slow, bumpy ride to Govan, there to wander streets where you could glance down towards the river and see steel turning into ships, towering high over the pavements, ships soon to be plying the seven seas. I loved it.

The early history of Fairfield's is well recorded in a heritage museum on site in Govan. The yard began more than 150 years ago as Randolph, Elder & Company and some years later it was run by John Elder himself who made a remarkable impact on the shipping industry with his work on the compound engine that increased fuel economy and hence profits for ship owners. After the Elder era it became, under William Pierce, the Fairfield Shipbuilding and Engineering Company. Many name changes followed as the ups and downs of recessions, world wars and industrial disputes affected the shipbuilding industry. The yard, at one time the largest and most successful on the Clyde, had many different public faces – in the seventies it was Govan Shipbuilders Ltd., and was part of the nationalised British Shipbuilders. Later it was also known as Kvaerner and in its current reincarnation it is part of the giant defence contractors BAE Systems. However much we may deplore the dilution of the independent nature of the yard there is certain aptness about its new role. Building for the navy was for many years a staple of the old Fairfield's. It is also apt that the yard saw its last conventional launch when *HMS Duncan,* the last of the type 45 destroyers, swished down greased ways into the narrow muddy waters of the Clyde. Now the new Queen Elizabeth class aircraft carriers are built in sections in construction halls, transferred by lowloader to huge barges and towed to other dockyards for assembly.

Fairfield's was a special yard. And it was in on the start of some of the most beautiful liners ever to be built. These were a sequence of white-hulled Empress style liners, which had a collective design that sticks in the memory. They had a long history starting around the turn of the last century. Canadian Pacific, the rail and shipping giant, wanted ships for the Liverpool–St Lawrence route. It was an era of mass immigration to the new world and Fairfield's *Empress of Britain* had lots of space for cheap third-class passengers and little of the glamour of later ships of the same name. This Empress served well in her designed role and as a trooper in the First World War before being scrapped in 1930. The Empress ships built in various yards are too many to mention individually but included such as the *Empress of Scotland,* the *Empress of Japan* and the *Empress of India.* When one vessel was scrapped another to carry the name was built. Not all were as beautiful as the latter ships but the immediate successor to Fairfield's Empress, also the *Empress of Britain,* was built by John Brown's in 1931 and was a more sophisticated ship with a remarkable top speed of the time of 24 knots. She also worked the Quebec route and briefly worked as a trooper at the start of the Second World War before a long-range German bomber spotted her off south-west Ireland in 1940. The attack left her crippled and drifting, to be finished off by a U32 with the loss of forty-nine lives. It was a sad end to a ship that had all the grace of today's super yachts despite the size difference. Incidentally it is a remarkable fact that in the month she was sunk, October 1940, the Allies lost fifty-seven ships in the north Atlantic and the Germans suffered the loss of only one U-boat.)

Fairfield's had a great reputation for naval ships. One of the most impressive was the battleship *HMS Howe*, the last of five King George V-class vessels. The design of this warship had an interesting history. Some four years after the end of the First World War international treaty restrictions were negotiated limiting the size of battleships in a well-intentioned, but in the end fruitless, effort to prevent a naval arms race. By the mid-thirties Japan and Italy had formally withdrawn from the treaty and it was obvious that international agreement was crumbling. The British government demonstrated its ability, still shown to this day, to play it by the rules no matter what beastly Johnny Foreigner was doing. The British realised that with the rise of Germany's naval might and that of other countries with warlike intentions, we were falling behind and new battleships needed to be built. But by this time the design was too far advanced to be changed and the King George V-class were built within the regulations that others ignored, in particular the main armament was 14-inch guns, far smaller than the then state of the art.

This failure was the fault of the politicians, not the shipbuilders and Fairfield's made the best of typical Admiralty bad decision making and built a warship that had an effective career though its design had been compromised. She was launched in the spring of 1940 but was not completed until the summer of 1942, a delay caused by the lack of raw materials: much-needed equipment and steel was urgently needed to upgrade the existing naval and civilian fleets. However, when ready for action *Howe* spent much time escorting and providing cover for Russian convoys in the Arctic. But after adventures in the icy waters of the north she saw action in the Med during the Allied invasion of Sicily. At the close of the Second World War in 1945 those 14-inch guns were in action in the Pacific providing naval bombardments during the Okinawa landings in April 1945. The Allied task force had a tough time in this bloody episode, in particular both American and British naval vessels were targets for kamikaze suicide bombers, but the *Howe* survived. Her final years were more mundane, mostly spent as the flagship of the Royal Naval training squadron at Portland and in 1961 she was broken up back in Scotland at Inverkeithing on the other side of the country from Fairfield's. There is, however, one permanent reminder of the *Howe* in St Giles' Cathedral in Edinburgh where the ship's bell is on display.

If the workers and management at Fairfield's were distressed at the design faults of the *Howe* it was not the first time they had been asked to build vessels that, no matter the skill and hard graft of those in the yards, were flawed from day one. At least the *Howe* and the other King George V-class, including the *Anson*, had a fairly successful war despite their faults. Not so the infamous K-class steam-powered (yes!) submarines that killed many of their crews and contributed little to the war effort other than to provoke sick laughter from outsiders looking at one of the most ill-conceived concepts in naval history. There is a parallel with the design of the *Howe* in that the Admiralty elite were out of touch with reality in the later years of the First World War. As was the case with the battleships to be used in the Second World War, the navy bigwigs belatedly realised that in the arms race Britain had been left behind. From their gilded offices in London and in the comfort of leather armchairs in their clubs, the men, and it was men only in those days, who ran the navy realised that as the Germans threw money and resources into a huge U-boat-building campaign we were still at the starting gate. Too late, as usual, we began to play catch up.

The idea was again well intentioned. Our new, if late on the scene, subs would be the fastest and the best. It was the method chosen involving steam power on the surface for speed that was bizarre if not downright daft. In my book *Scotland's Cruel Sea* (Black & White, Edinburgh, 2014) I quote the prominent American naval historian Edward C. Whitman who said of the decision to build the K-class:

> The Royal Navy's K-class submarines were perhaps the most badly conceived and ill-starred submersibles ever built by any nation. In both their original configuration and in several derivatives that followed, the K-boats compiled an almost unbroken record of disaster and death, unredeemed by even a single incident of combat effectiveness. Spawned by a flawed tactical concept, implemented with immature and dangerous technologies, and kept at sea by the Admiralty's stubborn refusal to admit the most obvious deficiencies the K-class left in their wake a fascinating tale of operational and technical folly for which the query, "What were they thinking?", has seldom been more appropriate.

If it had not been so tragic the whole project would have been more correctly labelled as farcical. Fairfield's and Scotland featured strongly in this epic of misadventure though the blame lay 500 or so miles further south. Right from the start there were indications that, as the song says, "there may be trouble ahead".

There is an interesting background to the fact that these subs had numbers rather than names. The nuclear subs of recent times have names that resonate with naval history like *Dreadnought, Valiant, Vanguard, Astute, Resolution, Courageous, Splendid, Sovereign,* and *Trafalgar* etc. (There are even committees to consider appropriate names. And they could find themselves in difficulties at times. In the early sixties there was controversy involving naval bigwigs and politicians over the use of *HMS Revenge* as a name. Some thought it insensitive and negative in that it implied the enemy had struck first, perhaps successfully. The then First Sea Lord Jellicoe liked the name a lot but even he thought that it might not be wise to use it for our first nuclear ballistic missile sub and in the end *HMS Resolution* was chosen and Revenge kept for one of the later vessels.) But the K-class vessels that killed so many brave submariners did not even have the dignity of a memorable name. It was different in the First World War. Maybe this was because of a feeling in the largely English upper class which ran the navy then that submarines were weapons to be ashamed of – creeping around underwater and torpedoing unarmed cargo vessels and particularly liners such as the *Lusitania* was just "not cricket". In contrast U-boat captains were popular heroes in the German Navy, often acclaimed for their efforts by the press. Tonnage sunk was the measure of success and a tendency to machine gun survivors in lifeboats or swimming for their lives in burning seas after a successful torpedo attack were ignored. Medals were thrown at U-boat captains like confetti by the Nazis. But back in "Blighty" in the First World War, no one gloried in the bravery and the exploits of the men who went to war under the waves.

Rather the reverse, for news of some of the K-class misadventures and loss of life were hidden from the ordinary reader, or indeed sailors in surface ships ("skimmers" as the submariners like to call them) and the absurdity of the design of the vessels and the mistaken thinking behind them kept something of a grim secret. You wonder if the real record of such vessels as the K-class had been well known, would crews be found to volunteer to serve in them? Despite a few at the top in the Admiralty at the time having reservations about them the subs were built. And on paper the statistics are impressive: almost 2,000 tons surfaced (2,566 submerged), 339 feet long with a beam of 26.5 feet and a draught of almost 21 feet. Propulsion: twin 10,500shp oil-fired boilers powering a geared steam turbine. Four powerful electric motors and an 800hp diesel generator for charging the batteries when surfaced. Up until the K-class came along surfaced sub speeds in the British Navy were around 16 knots but the new design exceeded that at around 21 knots or in some conditions even faster. But at what a cost? As the Americans observed, the entire fleet could not even mount one combat success. And before the keel of K13 (who isn't superstitious?) was laid there was a history of explosions, fuel leaks, boiler flashbacks and groundings.

You might have thought the Fairfield's version would at least be an improvement after the flaws demonstrated by the earlier version. Not so since the basic design was so flawed that tinkering around with it had no effect. The inescapable fact was that the design, in particular the use of funnels on the surface, would always make the subs subject to potentially fatal malfunction and human error. Rigging and unrigging the funnels was slow and dangerous with numerous "holes" in the hull to be closed and checked before a dive. If that wasn't enough, another ill thought out idea was using the oil-fired boilers that created high, almost unbearable, temperatures in the engine room. All sorts of ventilators were needed and this created another possible area of trouble, and possible ingress of seawater. Even the positioning of the boilers was a problem in that it made communication between the bow and stern parts of the sub difficult. It has to be said that in one area the K-class was a success – as previously mentioned they had a surface top speed of 23 knots which made them, for a time, the fastest subs in the world. The cost of this brief moment of glory, in terms of vessels and human lives lost, was however tragically high. The so-called super subs would more correctly be called killer subs.

The Govan yard got the order for K13 in August 1915 and the launch took place in November 1916. This submarine, and sadly many who sailed in her, faced a tragically short life. But, perhaps because the full facts were not known or appreciated, there appears to have been no fear of impending disaster when on 29 January 1917 at 8 a.m. the skipper, Commander Godfrey Herbert, gave the order to slip the moorings in Fairfield's and set sail on trials. Tugs pulled the giant sub out into the Clyde. Away from its birthplace and free at last the sub set downriver in calm waters, under its own power towards the test area in the Gare Loch. This was a day that had been planned for some time and the first early dive went well. It would not have been the navy of old if this was not followed by a "spot of decent lunch" which was said to have been enjoyed in "festive mood". There is no public suggestion that drink was involved in this disaster, but it would not have been a surprise to anyone with inside knowledge of the navy in the old days if it had. In a splendid history of the RN submarine service after the Second World War highly regarded historians Peter Hennessey and James Jinks remark in their book *The Silent Deep* on the long tradition of a heavy drinking culture in the navy, and in particular in the submarine service where, it has to be admitted, casualties were astonishingly high. There was danger in every dive. Once under the waves there was no guarantee of seeing the sky and breathing fresh air again. Thankfully the drinking problem was properly faced up to with the arrival of the nuclear age! Though from personal experience I can confirm that navy off-duty entertainment onshore and off can still have spectacular moments. There is additional supporting evidence of Hennessey and Jinks' comments on the pre-nuclear drinking habits of submariners in the previously mentioned memoir by Dan Conley. He does not name names but overdoing the grog even on duty was not confined to the lower ranks. Sobering stuff.

To be fair to the navy the misuse of alcohol was not unknown in the other services either. The caricature of overweight and red-faced senior army officers in their leather armchairs knocking back the port, and planning to send Tommies in the trenches in wildly optimistic attacks, was not without a grain of truth. Likewise I remember a widely respected member of the Scottish judiciary, a man who gained a reputation as a hammer of drink-drivers, recalling to me his days in the cockpit of a Fairy Swordfish taking off from aircraft carriers with a bottle of rum between his knees. He was well aware of the irony that he was to become the scourge of errant motorists. But as he pointed out he was engaged in battle with a dangerous enemy and there was no certainty that he would return from a foray over the oceans alive. Somewhat different from the criminals who would drink and threaten the lives of other innocent motorists on the road.

Back to the K-class. At 3.15 p.m. with the decent lunch over it was back to the dive area for a routine test of instruments, an exercise that initially seemed to have gone well. But one instrument was flickering, a happening that was put down to a wiring fault. In fact it was indicating a problem with the boiler room ventilators (necessary to cool an area that was almost unworkable in because of the heat and the situation of the equipment). Investigations after the fatal malfunction indicated that four of the air vents had not been properly closed as the sub began to submerge. The plan was to level out at the shallow depth of 6 metres, but this did not happen and the vessel continued to dive deeper. Frantic efforts were made to stop the plunge with the hydroplanes moved quickly to the "hard-a-rise" position in an effort to get back to the surface. Everyone aboard knew they were in trouble as the sub was filled with the noise of screaming compressed air clearing the ballast tanks of tons of water. News that the boiler room was flooding was swiftly conveyed to the officers as the seamen fought off panic – tons of sea was pouring into the hull at high speed through the faulty ventilator system.

The officers trying to control a frightening situation now faced the hardest of decisions to come to a commander. But there was no way of avoiding the correct conclusion. The watertight doors between the boiler room and the rest of the vessel had to be slammed shut and fast. It meant certain death for those on the wrong side of the doors, but if action was not taken there was no hope for any one aboard, naval personnel or shipyard workers helping with the trials. The commander ordered the doors shut. Thirty-one men went to an agonising death. This was only the start of a desperate situation. The sub's uncontrolled dive had gone on and in the end it settled stern down in 15 metres of water. Those who survived on the right side of the watertight doors were now trapped with a limited air supply. And even this was threatened when a sudden burst of oxygen-consuming flame sprang out of a switchboard. This was quickly put out by frantic efforts of the trapped men, but not before it had taken away some of the breathable air.

All this desperate action was invisible to those on shore who were unaware of the drama in the fairly shallow waters of the loch. But K13's failure to reappear eventually caused alarm. It took around seven hours, until 10 p.m., for the first rescue vessel to arrive on the scene and it had taken six hours during which the trapped men were breathing a limited supply of oxygen before tugs were sent to the scene. (An oddity is that on this first dive it seems the sub was not properly escorted by rescue vessels.) The first rescue boat was the *Gossamer*, an elderly gunboat, and clearly a priority was to send down divers to assess the situation. No suitable diving suit was on the *Gossamer* and when one was finally found it was so perished it almost drowned the volunteer who put it on. Eventually a civilian diver from the builders, Fairfield's, managed to reach the sunken hull and communicated with the trapped men by hammering out messages in Morse code. He reported that the bottom was soft and sandy and that the sub had hit it at some speed despite the fact that the ballast keel had been jettisoned. This was to be a further problem later.

Meanwhile under the dark waters of the loch various escape plans were talked through. There were two commanders on board, Captain Godfrey Herbert and Captain Francis Goodhart, the highly rated officer slated to command the next sub in the line, K14, who already had had a good war in submarines, as they say in the services. It seemed a good idea to try to get a man on the surface with knowledge of the inside of the sub so that he could help rescuers. It was a dangerous plan but, dicey or not, it was considered a first way forward and Goodhart volunteered to escape through the conning tower propelled upwards by a burst of compressed air. Herbert was to remain in overall charge. But as final preparations were made a burst of compressed air took Goodhart by surprise and forced him at high speed on to the steel of the conning tower and he died instantly. Goodhart was subsequently awarded the Albert medal and this short quote from the full official citation illustrated his bravery:

> After several hours the only prospect of saving those remaining on board appeared to be for someone to escape from the submarine in order to concert measures with the rescuers, who were by this time present on the surface. Commander Goodhart, after consultation with the Commanding Officer, volunteered to make the attempt. Accordingly, after placing in his belt a small tin cylinder with instructions for the rescuers, Commander Goodhart went into the conning tower with the Commanding Officer. The conning tower was flooded up to their waists, and the high-pressure air was turned on; the clips of the conning tower were knocked off and the conning tower lid was soon wide open. Commander Goodhart then stood up in the dome, took a deep breath, and made his escape, but, unfortunately, was blown by the pressure of air against part of the super-structure, and was killed by the force of the blow. The Commanding Officer, whose intention it had been to return inside the submarine after Commander Goodhart's escape, was involuntarily forced to the surface by the air pressure, and it was thus rendered possible for the plans for rescuing those still inside the submarine to be carried out.

It was lucky for the crew, too, that Herbert survived, for, as the citation noted, his knowledge of the inside of the sub was really helpful to the rescue effort. The main thing now was to calculate how much air was left in the sub and how long it would last. The answer was not scientific but chilling – "not long". It was now a race against time to get the men to the surface before they choked to death as the oxygen ran out.

Divers were sent back down and hammers and Morse

code again came into play. They managed this time to connect a small hose to a tube through which some air, food and drink was passed. Playing cards were also passed through to help the trapped men cope with their perilous situation. What to do next was the problem and a plan was devised to feed hawsers round the bow of the sub, which was pointing upwards, and winch it up above water level. Commander Herbert then thought the survivors could escape through the forward torpedo tubes. At first all went well and the bow began to get to the surface, but when success was looking likely the hull suddenly slipped back under the waves. The only alternative now was for divers to cut through the hull itself, a dangerous and time-consuming operation under water. But, as the air inside was running out, there was a breakthrough into the hull and the forty-eight survivors escaped to the surface to gasp in fresh air. They had been trapped for fifty-seven hours, an incredible ordeal.

The death toll from this plunge to the bottom by one of the most ill designed of submarine classes was thirty-two. This was a figure that included six civilians from Fairfield's itself, something that caused great anguish to their families and fellow workers and friends in the Govan area. When the grim task of removing the bodies of the victims was complete there was a shock. It was thought that there would be thirty-two corpses (Commander Goodhart's body was trapped in the conning tower) but in fact only twenty-nine were found. Remarkable as it seems, two crewmen had managed to escape from the rear of the sub as it sank. It is sad to record that during the daylight hours after the sinking a maid in a local hotel had reported seeing two men in the water, but the authorities took no notice. Had they acted both men might have been found alive. The body of one man was taken from the sea months later but his companion was never found. The story of the K-class has never received the attention it deserved, the folly of its design and the lives it claimed overshadowed by newspaper reports of the slaughter in the trenches of mainland Europe and the exploits of the early fliers. But Govan folk, who worked in the yards and lived in the nearby tenements, and their descendants, will never forget.

Three impressive memorials were built to honour the dead. The one most familiar to Clydesiders was erected in Elder Park, Govan; a rivet's throw from the spot K13 was built. It was erected some years after the disaster and the end of the war to end all wars. Fairfield's workers contributed to the cost and at the unveiling ceremony Sir Alexander Kennedy paid a moving tribute to those who died in what was still, seemingly without irony, described as a "super sub". Much of the detail of what had happened had never been exposed to public scrutiny because of war secrecy, but now *The Glasgow Herald*, as it then was, was able to report: "Owing to an overlook on the part of someone who paid for his mistake with his life, four large ventilators leading to the boiler room were left open." Clearly there was human error in the operation but there was no newspaper condemnation of the human error in the Admiralty that conceived and built what was in effect a series of death traps. Sir Alexander did however have some deserved praise for Govan folk. Of those who worked in the yard he said: "They lost their lives when engaged in the testing of a naval weapon which had been constructed for the purpose of overcoming our enemies and securing national safety."

There is also a memorial to the men who died at the entrance to the Faslane naval base, current home to Britain's nuclear subs. And thousands of miles away there is another memorial at Carlingford, New South Wales, Australia. This was paid for by the widow of Charles Freestone, a leading telegraphist on K13, who survived and after the war started a new life in Australia. Unveiled in September 1961 it has a water feature and cairn higher than a man. The inscription to K13 reads: "This memorial has been created in memory of those officers and men of the Commonwealth who gave their lives while serving the cause of freedom."

And what of K13 itself? It was refloated and refitted and renamed K22. The name change brought no luck as the sub was one of the casualties in what became known as the Battle of May Island. This tale of incompetence and disaster is now, almost a hundred years after it happened, largely forgotten. This was a battle with no foreign force – the enemy was the inability of the Royal Navy to complete an exercise in the North Sea safely. Off the Fife coast warships large and small and several submarines were in collisions on a dark and misty night. Historians often talk of "the fog of war" obscuring the facts and this was a classic case. Not only did a real sea fog contribute to the disaster but in the aftermath the story of what really happened was hidden behind swirling mists of misinformation and conjecture. The navy's excuse of not spelling out what happened was the usual one – in a time of war, giving the public the full facts of such an incident would damage public confidence in the armed forces and those who led them. In particular there is no convincing agreement on the number of seafarers who died. It seems certainly to have reached three figures (the lowest estimate I have seen is 104) though a story in *The Guardian* newspaper in 2011 put it as high as 270.

The accident, or series of accidents, happened on the night of 31 January to 1 February 1918. A force of around forty vessels, submarines and surface vessels large and small left the Rosyth area for pre-planned exercises in the North Sea. They steamed on the surface in a convoy almost 30 miles long. The K-class, some of which had recently been redeployed from Scapa Flow, was well represented. The convoy included cruisers and smaller warships and a group of K3, K4, K6 and K7 led by *HMS Fearless* and another led by *HMS Ithuriel* (K11, K12, K14, K17 and K22, formerly K13.) The fear that there was a German U-boat presence in the area meant that there was radio silence between ships and subs and the convoy proceeded in the dark with helmsmen steering at the weak stern lights of the ship in front.

There was black humour in calling the episode "The Battle of May Island". The "Deadly Farce off May Island" would have been a more accurate headline. The chaos and sinkings began when lights were seen approaching the subs as the convoy picked up speed. The unidentified lights prompted the squadron of subs to turn sharply to port though it turned out later that the lights were from naval minesweepers not any feared German force. As this happened another K-class mechanical failure triggered fatal collisions – K14's helm jammed and she veered out of position. She and the sub immediately behind her had to turn on navigating lights in an effort to see what was happening. The dodgy steering was eventually freed and K14 managed to get back in line but Fairfield's K22 had lost sight of the many vessels around and collided with K14. Both subs were left drifting and helpless as the convoy surged on in the mist, individual ships unaware of the chaos around them. In such a desperate situation radio silence was broken and K22 indicated that it thought it could reach port despite the damage. K14 was sinking fast. The commander of K22 had been a tad optimistic. She was smashed into by the battle cruiser ironically named *HMS Inflexible*. This blow was of such force that it bent the first 30 feet or so at right angles and she settled down into the water with only the conning tower above the waves. A night of horror was ending. The majority of the fatalities occurred on K4 (fifty-five) and K17 (forty-seven) though there were others never properly quantified as a result of collisions, some minor, some serious. Some seamen attempting to swim to safety were cut down in the water by naval vessels thrashing round in the darkness and confusion. So ended the dramatic, tragic and uncelebrated life of perhaps the only vessel built in the legendary Govan yard that was doomed to infamy from the very moment of laying the first steel by the incompetence of its designers. Kalamity class indeed!

8

A Long Life from Arran Speedster to Minesweeper and Back

While that submarine disaster was a bump in the generally smooth and successful story of Fairfield's shipbuilding history, the original owners of the yard also had some not too smooth moments. Fairfield Shipbuilding & Engineering Company Limited, Govan, Glasgow, to give it its Sunday name, was the successor to Randolph, Elder & Co. and John Elder & Co. John Elder was a remarkable marine engineer and shipbuilder. His main claims to fame were that he developed practical compounding marine engines and that he was a pioneer of the integrated shipbuilding yard. His engines were vital ingredients in speeding up the move from sail to steam. But perhaps more important was the fact that he introduced in his Govan yard, now still in use as part of BAE Systems, something of the production line engineering ideas used later in the motor industry by such as Henry Ford. The yard now produces sections of the new Queen Elizabeth aircraft carrier class. When completed these sections – built in six yards – are towed by barge to Roysth for assembly. A bit different from the old ways but practical when building the Royal Navy's biggest ships. Even in Govan today you can see something of the visionary developments in shipbuilding that are down to John Elder. It is remarkable to think that as long ago as 1869 this site was the workplace for 4,000 people and produced thousands of tons of shipping and engines that were the most powerful in the world. Little wonder that he is still a legend in Govan. The great multinational companies today seem to have more concern for dodging tax than the welfare of the communities in which they prosper. That is an accusation that could not be made about John Elder, who earned the respect of his workers. A cleric writing about his funeral reported that "a very army of workmen followed his body". In those class-conscious days gone by the writer noted that the workmen were "dressed like gentlemen", a serious mark of their respect. A statue was erected in his memory by public subscription in Elder Park, Govan (where else?) and the inscription in part reads: "His unwearied efforts to promote the welfare of the working classes, his integrity of character, firmness of purpose, and kindness of heart, claim equally with his genius, enduring remembrance." Amen to that.

But even in this hive of activity and enterprise, and amid all its success, Elder's yard had at least one eccentric aberration, though it all happened after his death, at the early age of forty-five in 1869. Glasgow's famous Museum of Transport had an impressive section devoted to ship models held in various sites before finally moving to its iconic new building on the riverside. In particular, noses pressed against glass cases, generations of youngsters spent dreich Sunday afternoons in Kelvingrove Art Galleries admiring immaculately detailed models of ships. In many instances the youngsters were looking at ships that their dads, grandfathers and uncles had helped build. In one glass case I remember there was a model to rival steam-powered submarines in idiosyncrasy. This was an almost circular steam yacht, the *Livadia*.

It has been described as "a gigantic life-size experiment". As steam and iron replaced wood and sail there was a tendency among naval architects to decrease length and widen beam, a move that protected the maximum internal equipment with the minimum of side armour. It was also thought that a near circular shape would control the motion caused by swells. Russia took a lead in this and Vice Admiral Andry Popov developed the idea to its extreme – more or less round battleships. A couple were built and they had the advantage of shallow draft suitable to many of the waters the Russian Navy operated in. But that was the only good point. The drag caused by a wide hull was too much for the engines, seagoing ability was horrific with huge flat bottoms causing endless damage by waves hammering against the ship, and sailing down a tidal stream, steering was almost impossible. You can't help but reflect that an hour or so with a model and the use of a ship tank would have saved the bother of such a "life-size experiment". In fact a Dutch naval architect did conduct a few tests with a paraffin wax model in a basin and came to the erroneous conclusion that the design might work. He was a tad optimistic to say the least. Another defect was that the round vessels were too wide to fit into existing docks for repairs.

Popov continued to believe in round ships despite the troubles of the earlier navy versions and when the House of Romanov were on the hunt for a new Royal Yacht he proposed a round version as a prototype for new battle-ships. Elder's in Govan got the contract to build the ship in 1879. There was a conventional superstructure laid on top of a hull that resembled the shape of a turbot. By this time even Popov had realised a truly circular ship was just not going to work. He had compromised with a length of 79 metres and a beam of 47 metres. As befits a royal yacht the interior was luxurious. The *Livadia* performed better than expected and in some sea conditions was more comfortable than a conventional ship, but as mentioned the flat bottom was prone to damage caused by wave slamming. Unlike our *Britannia* which served its purpose well for years this royal yacht was only used once in its intended role carrying a couple of grand dukes across the Black Sea in impressive luxury. But Alexander II, perhaps fed up with the constant problems and faced with terrorist and other more pressing political problems, had decided the flawed ship was a waste of time and money and as early as 1881 her engines were stripped out and reused on Russian cruisers leaving behind a rusting hulk that was a far cry from the imperial glory of *Livadia* on launch day.

The launch had been a spectacular affair even for the Clyde. It was calculated that 10,000 spectators watched and Grand Duke Alexey had travelled from Russia. The early speculation that the so-called "experiment" was a proto- type for new battleships was now big news in the press and many were unhappy that we should be helping the Russians. The experiment jibe may have been true of the hull, but the furnishings were far from experimental: recep- tion rooms were decorated in Louis XIV style, "Crimean- Tartar" style for drawing rooms, and private rooms were made out in a kind of fake English upper class style. But in the end it was the failure of the round hull to stand up to the battering of heavy seas that doomed the dream of round ships. It ended badly for the *Livadia* and Popov – who was at one time accused of fraud because his ship had not delivered on its promises of performance, in particular speed, and that doomed the project. If it was ever possible for a ship to sail up a dead end, the *Livadia* did it. But at least it gave Glasgow youngsters something to do to help pass a rainy Sunday!

Another favourite museum model was that of the Fairfield's-built *Jeanie Deans.* Only the incomparable *Waverley* surpassed this Clyde steamer in its longevity in public memory. Interesting that both took their names from the work of Walter Scott. In the heyday of trips "doon the watter", as Firth of Clyde holidays became known, the *Jeanie* was the number one choice of aficionados of the pleasure fleets. She had a long and eventful life after launching in Govan in 1931. In her days on the Clyde one of her major attractions was her speed – a zippy 18.5 knots at full power. Even today the day trippers and tourists who queue to join the *Waverley* for a trip down the river, now passing many yards long closed and their memories condemned to the history books, remark how speedy she is at around the same maximum speed as the *Jeanie Deans.* Unlike the *Waverley* the *Jeanie Deans* could not escape the threat of the breaker's yard and was dismantled in Belgium in 1967. Today, half a century later, most of the non deep-sea shipping traffic on the Clyde is provided by CalMac and Western Ferries car ferries. Regularity and the ability to operate all year round is more important than speed, something that irks the good folk of Arran who would prefer something a tad faster than a mere 15 knots to take them on trips to the mainland. They remember the old speedier passenger ferries with affection.

In the thirties and after the Second World War speed was the thing. Piers such as the old one at Dunoon were often thick with potential passengers looking for a sail, no destination in particular, just a sail, and the steamers of the day often raced each other to get to an empty berth first to pick up the traffic. When the *Jeanie Deans* was designed fast turbine steamers were threatening the paddlers, but her owners, the London and North Eastern Railway, wanted vessels with a shallow draft allowing them to call at Craigendoran and Helensburgh on the north side of the river. There had been an earlier *Jeanie Deans*, built by Barclay, Curle & Co., which had a long career on the Clyde and Lough Foyle until it was broken up in 1920. So the name was a familiar one. That impressive speed of the new *Jeanie* came from the fact that she was the first Clyde steamer with a three-crank engine. Originally she had an open bridge and twin funnels. After a year or so in operation it was felt there was insufficient shelter on deck for passengers in poor weather. The solution was a large first-class observation saloon built forward. Another noticeable defect was that the funnels had a tendency to deposit hot cinders on the paying passengers (something rail passengers in the age of steam knew well). The funnels were made taller to ameliorate the problem.

In the thirties the *Jeanie Deans* did not venture much down the estuary, concentrating instead on LNER's key summer destinations of Lochgoilhead and Arrochar. But as the years passed, there were Sunday excursions down towards the open sea at Ayr and cruises round Ailsa Craig.

The versatility of the Clyde yards is demonstrated by the fact that when the *Jeanie Deans* was built at Fairfield's upriver at Govan, the little vessel slotted in between the construction of mighty naval vessels and such as the beautiful Empress liners. The folksy name of this famous pleasure vessel has contributed to its high place in the list of steamers that resonate with Glaswegians. Walter Scott's characters were certainly a gift to anyone looking for an attractive, unusual name. Jeanie herself, an upright and highly religious character, would have been surprised that even pubs were named after her, never mind a pleasure steamer. Others to use the name were railway locomotives and there was even an opera, a play and a poem of that name.

When operating out of Craigendoran, her regular route took her to nearby Helensburgh and round the corner, as it were, up to Arrochar at the head of Loch Long to berth in the shadow of the famous Arrochar Alps, a magnificent sight, especially in the winter snow.

In her later life the *Jeanie* was in competition for the "doon the watter" traffic with the newer, fast and stylish, sister turbine steamers the *Duchess of Hamilton* and *Duchess of Montrose*. These two legendary Clyde steamers did not have the shallow water operational ability of the traditional paddle steamers. But, fast and beautiful, they had something of a private yacht aura about them. As a youngster I made regular trips to Campbeltown on both of these ships and knew first hand of their comfort and good looks as I roamed them both, on open deck and below, as my father did his usual thorough job of inspecting the bars and dining saloons! As a violinist himself he also appreciated the accordion band who wandered the decks entertaining the passengers with some suitable Scottish music or maybe a rendering of the current best-selling tunes on offer in the specialist music shops, selling sheet music, 78s and a selection of instruments that proliferated in Glasgow at the time. The customers who had spent most time in the ship's bars and restaurants were the first to show their appreciation and generosity when the hat came round. I remember seeing some of the more uninhibited "Glesca" ladies on a day out enjoying a dance to the jaunty sound of the ship's band. Maybe a wee sherry or two had been taken. Incidentally, the facilities on the Duchesses, each catering for almost 2,000 passengers when at capacity, included an "Old English" pub, several spacious lounges and a tasty menu in the restaurant.

When the Second World War broke out the *Jeanie Deans* was unchallenged as the longest and fastest paddler on the Clyde and an attractive proposition for the government to requisition into the forces. "Called up", the *Jeanie* survived dangerous years as a minesweeper and an anti-aircraft ship on the River Thames helping to clear the London skies of Nazi aircraft. After the war it was back to more mundane work on the Clyde though by now the folk of the area and tourists from the south had developed a great affection for this sturdy little veteran. Around this time she was refitted as an oil burner and that newly developed wartime lifesaver, a radar, fitted. But modernised or not, time was running out for the old lady of the Clyde and she was sold and renamed *Queen of the South* for pleasure sailings on her old wartime haunt, the Thames. The venture was blighted by technical problems and the breaker's yard beckoned.

A very different vessel much remembered by old Fairfield's workers came to a tragic end on the other side of the world – the roll-on roll-off ferry *Wahine*. Several guys who worked in the yard in the sixties told me they thought the design of this New Zealand ferry was, to their eye, not quite as robust as it could have been. But design and construction was not to blame for New Zealand's most famous maritime disaster. Fifty-three people, out of more than 700 on board, died when the ferry went down. It was not the largest number of lives lost at sea in these islands in accidents, but it is the most remembered simply because the drama, unlike most sea incidents, was caught live on TV and radio and watched worldwide.

After her launch in Govan she sailed from Greenock for New Zealand on 18 June 1966 arriving at Wellington shortly before the end of July and she was in service a mere week after her arrival. Safety was supposedly built in to her with fourteen watertight compartments, eight fibreglass lifeboats that could each hold fifty people and six of what were called standard life boats, each 31 feet long and capable of holding ninety-nine people. In addition there were thirty-six inflatable life rafts. Yet this well constructed and well equipped vessel capsized and sank just a short distance from the shore and the suburbs of Wellington. Those who died either drowned or succumbed to exposure or injuries caused during the panic and attempts at evacuation.

As is often the case in disasters, the cause was a combination of circumstances. Well found as she was, the *Wahine* was no match for the weather on the day she capsized. On the early hours of 10 April 1968, two violent storm fronts met over the city of Wellington creating a single extratropical cyclone that was the worst in New Zealand's history. Cyclone Giselle, not a particularly apt name for a killer you might think, moving south hit the city just as another storm arrived from Antarctica. The winds reached 171 miles an hour, the worst ever recorded. On land in one suburb alone 100 roofs were whipped off houses. Ambulances and trucks trying to reach the injured were blown on to their sides. Out at sea the situation was unimaginable.

There is a striking similarity in the tale of the *Wahine* to what happened to the *Princess Victoria* off the Scottish coast some years earlier. As with the *Princess Victoria* when the ferry set sail there were weather warnings but they did not predict the full fury of what was about to happen. And like Captain Donaldson of the *Princess Victoria*, Captain Robertson was well used to rough weather in his patch, in this case the Cook Straight.

At 5.50 a.m. the winds had risen, whipping up unprecedented seas but Captain Robertson decided to try to enter Wellington harbour despite the weather. White water thundered down on the *Wahine* and she lost the use of her radar. One gigantic wave pushed her off course and she headed towards the rocks known as Barrett Reef. Captain Robertson was unable to turn her around in the winds and decided to back her out to sea – another similarity with the *Princess Victoria*. But she was not answering the helm and had lost control of her engines. At 6.40 a.m. the battle was really beginning in earnest – she struck the tip of the reef. This was near the harbour and less than a mile from the shore. Her hull was breeched below the waterline and a propeller torn off. Meanwhile the winds continued at around 160 mph. The passengers donned lifejackets and scrambled to muster stations.

After three hours or so anchors which had been deployed and failed to hold her finally got a grip of the ground close to the shore at a spot called Seaton. A tug did reach her, but attempts at towing her to safety failed. As did other attempts including the efforts of a pilot boat which reached the scene. At this stage even in the storm the full danger was not apparent. After all she was in water only around 30 feet deep. It was after 1 p.m. when wind and tide turned *Wahine* around into a patch of clear water. But she suddenly listed to the point of no return and the order to abandon ship was given. But, as has happened before in other accidents, only the lifeboats on one side of the ship could be used, so severe was the list. Some did get launched on the starboard side and some lucky passengers reached the shore on vastly overcrowded boats. Others perished when life rafts capsized and, when the ship finally actually sank, hundreds were swept into the rough seas.

The inevitable inquiry found that errors of judgement had been made but account was also taken of the remark-able weather. It said that had the order to abandon ship been given earlier or later, more lives would have been lost. A "window" to launch the lifeboats had been correctly used. Officers and crew found charges against them had been raised but all were acquitted. So ended, thousands of miles from Govan, the life of a Clydebuilt vessel that in its time was one of the largest and most successful of the world's growing fleets of Ro-Ro ships. Cyclone Giselle had defeated her.

9

Sparks and Flying Rivets –
The Hard Life of the "Hudder Oan"

To less tragic memories: Fairfield's was always at the forefront of innovation in the yards, including the transition
from riveted to welded steel hulls. A vital cog in the wheel
of the riveting process was what was called the "hudder
oan". The rivets themselves were heated till they glowed
red hot and then plucked by tongs out of the flames and
in one swift rhythmic movement skilfully held at the right
angle and in the right spot by the "hudder oan". His mate
then hammered it home in a shower of sparks and a wall
of sound. Many years ago in a Cambuslang pub I was
given a first-hand word picture of this by one of the most
remarkable men in the history of the Clyde yards – Sammy
Gilmore of the Upper Clyde Shipbuilders fame. (More of
this elsewhere in this book.) Sammy was part of the famous
boxing family dynasty, the Gilmours. The difference in the
spelling is no error. Even in the middle of the last century
there was still bad blood between Catholics and Protestants
in Scotland and sometimes it was wise not to be too upfront
about which side of the divide you were on. The Gilmores,

like many a Glasgow family, had their roots in Ireland. And the founder of the dynasty that dominated boxing in Scotland for decades, the "Auld Yin" Jim Gilmour, had decided to use the more Scottish version of the name as he judged that having the Irish spelling, Gilmore, and its religious connotations, on a ticket might not be of great sales value!

I would have thought the "hudder oan" was a job putting strength at a premium. Sammy Gilmore, the cousin of Tommy Gilmour, the grandson of Jim and perhaps Scotland's greatest-ever boxing promoter, put me right. He told me that when the "Auld Yin", who had boxed at the Olympics, had worked in Fairfield's his long hours of training in the gym had left him too "muscle-bound" for the job. Throwing around red-hot rivets, catching them and placing them where needed required you to be fast on your feet and lithe; mere strength was not enough. Interestingly, during the manpower shortage on the home front women excelled at this job, taking to catching red-hot rivets in their stride.

In the yards in his day, though, Jim could put his fighting powers to good use if needed. Shipyard workers, then and now, like a bet. And they had a lot of energy despite the hard nature of the job. Away from the riverside in other factories this excess might have been worked off in lunch-time games of football with jackets and jerseys as goalposts. Fairfield's did not approve of this and it was banned and as a consequence there were often two or more pitch-and-toss games going on in between eating the traditional "jeely piece" and swigging tea out of fire-blackened tin cans. Running such gambling suited old Jim – his skill with his fists and his reputation made him the perfect controller of the hard cash that swilled around during the lunch break. It was in Fairfield's that he honed his skills as a bookmaker, a career that in the end was to be more cash productive than helping to build ships.

Glasgow and the Clydeside towns are, as earlier noted, littered with architectural reminders of the great days – sad, and sometimes overgrown and weed-infested, remnants of the great days that are over. One such place was the old Harland and Wolff engineering shed in Govan. After Harland and Wolff closed their Glasgow operation in 1962 to concentrate investment on their Belfast yard the shed had a brief new life in show business, perhaps apt since it was located not far from the current Pacific Quay media complex. The two most memorable productions in this unusual venue for live theatre were *The Ship* and *The Big Picnic* (though ex-Clydeside shipyard workers like Billy Connolly and Nicholas Parsons might tell you that every day in a yard was live real-life theatre!) *The Ship* in 1990 was a tribute to the folk history of those who toiled in the yards, written and directed by Bill Bryden, and *The Big Picnic* was the same writer's take on the horror of First World War trench battles with the wonderful Jimmy Logan taking a leading role. Clearly the venue was suitable for the first, for the second its attraction was less obvious, but in promotional literature for Promenade Productions Bryden wrote:

We decided to lay out a section of the wasteland exploiting the great size of our shed/theatre, because its very length of 250 feet was no more than the amount of ground sometimes gained after days of fighting which often cost thousands of lives. To utilise this epic space to the full, we again adopted the promenade style, where the audience move with the action so that they too advance along the 250 feet and retreat and advance again and retreat again before the day is over. The other element in our wasteland is our version of the old theatrical device known as the *deus ex machina* or the god of the machine, which in seven-teenth-century theatre lowered in the gods and the goddesses. In our version, we have reinstated the bridge crane as used when the shed was first built and which rides on the original rails that can carry over fifty tons. This mobile crane represents the remorseless, inhuman tide of destruction as it cruises back and forth, like a great bird scavenging over the battlefield. Its central icon is the Angel of Death, here called the Angel of Mons. She is a distillation of the many (over 10,000) sightings and mass hallucinations reported by allied soldiers, who saw visions of angels and folk heroes, saints and lost relatives in the sky over the Western Front. For us, she is the arbitrary hand of fate and the bringer of release from this hell.

I saw the show on a cold and dreich autumn evening, the sort of bone chilling climate that Glasgow seems to specialise in. But I was mesmerised by the production in which the use of space as described above was imaginative and successful without diluting the emotion of it all. You would have been stone-hearted and stupid not to have been affected by such a night of theatre. Tears flowed. Mind you, I also remember the chill winds that drifted inside the vast hall with its cold uncovered walls so unlike the red velvet, gold leaf furnishing and central heating of conventional theatre spaces.

The Shed, and that brief late life in the show business spotlight, is only a tiny part of a tumbledown collection of rusting cranes, assembly sheds, engine works, empty dry docks, rope works and old unused landing stages that fester on both banks of the Clyde. In their own way these relics still standing amid new housing estates and shopping malls are impressive enough to give the modern visitor some under-standing of what a massive industry shipbuilding was in its heyday. But it is hard for even a student of maritime matters to take in completely the sheer complexity and size of the industry. The firms Harland and Wolff, William Beardmore & Co. and Fairfield's are only the most prominent of the Govan yards. The Clydebuilt Database lists almost 3,000 ships built in this one small area of Glasgow (though the Govan folk to this day, like their compatriots upriver in Rutherglen, like to protest an independence from the city). The list of manufacturers apart from the most famous mentioned includes: Robert Napier & Company, Elder & Company, Dobbie, Hedderwick & McGaw, Dobie & Company, Mackie & Thomson, Smith & Rodger, London & Glasgow Engineering and Iron Shipbuilding Company, John Elder and Company, Alexander Stephens & Sons, J. & G. Thomson. There are more.

All this in a relatively small area, but an area with an impressive history before the days of ocean-going sailing ships, never mind liners or warships and submarines.

There is a great Christian connection: the first references to Govan itself are of a religious nature. In 1136 when Glasgow Cathedral was consecrated, King David gave the See lands in Govan and in Partick, across the river. The town was on the map. In 1759 the locals arranged for the deepening of the Clyde and the reclamation of channels on the then shallow river. This was to lead to the growth of shipbuilding. There was a dye works and silk mill in the burgh. It was all something of a rural idyll with houses on the famous Water Row with thatched roofs. Labour leader Keir Hardie was said to have lived in Water Row, though by that time heavy industry had moved in and changed the look of the place and the way of life. The size of the independent Govan in the years before it was annexed by Glasgow in 1912 is now largely forgotten by Glaswegians, most of whom would be surprised to learn it was then the seventh largest town in Scotland.

Industrialisation brought wealth to the yard owners, but much poverty and deprivation to the area. Mind you, some of this came about when in the thirties families were moved out of the overcrowded and under-cared-for Gorbals. We don't seem to learn the lessons of history in Scotland for much the same thing happened in the fifties when Gorbals folk again found themselves decanted, this time to vast new housing estates with few social facilities – "deserts with windaes" as one comic aptly put it. Back in the old days in Govan one new housing estate was jokingly known as "Wine Alley". Latterly there were problems with drug abuse and unemployment.

But nothing can take away Govan's place in history as the birthplace of modern iron shipbuilding. The man behind this was Robert Napier, often referred to as the "Father of Clyde Shipbuilding", a man mentioned in other parts of this book. Napier had taken over an old Govan wooden shipbuilding yard in 1841 and later expanded into other yards making a name for himself with the quality of his products.

He had an early connection with Cunard and built the Royal Navy's first iron paddle steamers and other famous warships, including the ironclad *HMS Black Prince*. Like others on the Clyde he was not afraid of innovation and his yard built the world's first ferry capable of carrying trains, in this case across the Firth of Forth in the mid nineteenth century, and was given the rather grand title of the world's first "floating railway". The *Leviathan* sailed between Granton and Burntisland and continued to operate until 1890 when the first Forth Bridge opened. From summer 2017 the crossing will be made on one of the three magnificent and iconic bridges, the old rail bridge, the handsome road bridge and the spectacular new Queensferry Crossing, which is globally unique, the longest three-tower, cable-stayed bridge in the world at almost two miles. The engineering facts are impressive as is the beauty of what has been created, something that is not always the case in the world of construction. The three bridges make up a global tourist attraction in themselves as well as getting folk from one side of the firth to the other.

When Napier died in 1876 the yards were bought by a former apprentice A. C. Kirk and when he died the famous Beardmore engineering firm took over and moved operations to nearby Dalmuir. Then in 1912 Harland and Wolff moved into Govan. Initially with great success. One of the drivers behind the move was political instability in Northern Ireland at the time. Not much changes. On the purchase the company set about amalgamating neighbouring yards and creating a massive facility with no less than seven building berths, a fitting out basin and sprawling workshops. The yard had the distinction of being the furthest from the open sea than any other major Clyde yard, though this did not seem to hinder it since in its heyday it employed around 6,000 people. The early expansion continued with the purchase of A. & J. Inglis in 1919. The company also had a stake in the famous Lanarkshire steel maker Colville's. In addition they had yards in Liverpool, London and Southampton. But with British shipbuilders in trouble in the sixties, losing work to other, often state-subsidised shipbuilders worldwide, Harland and Wolff closed those operations and retreated to its main base in Belfast, most remembered as the birthplace of the so-called unsinkable *Titanic*. Now Northern Ireland's biggest city has created a museum to the most famous ship built there called the Titanic Experience and it has quickly gained a fine reputation as a world-class maritime museum and is a major tourist attraction.

Earlier in this book Denny's flirtation with aircraft production was mentioned. Harland and Wolff made similar attempt to move from the seas to the skies. Their plane-making subsidiary, unimaginatively called Short and Harland, in Belfast, is a tad more remembered than aircraft production on the Clyde. Short's first order in 1936 was for no less than 189 Handley Page bombers and in the Second World War it also built Short Stirling bombers and in peacetimes a range of small commercial aircraft including the rather ugly, but successful, Skyvan.

In its closing days on the Clyde, Harland specialised in tankers and motor ships. Twelve tankers were built for British Petroleum. The "B" class motor ships built for the British India Company were remarkable for their elegance. Some maritime enthusiasts even wrote that these hard-working commercial vessels were "yacht-like" which might be going a bit far, but certainly these ships were far removed from the popular perception of the ageing rust-bucket tramp steamers that in earlier times had ranged the oceans searching out any old cargo they could find. Amid all the ships built in Govan by Harland there was an interesting curiosity of an early aircraft carrier.

The *Empire MacKay* was what was more properly known as a MAC ship (merchant aircraft carrier). She had a short flat top deck from which aircraft, mostly biplanes, could manage to run along gathering just enough speed to stagger into the air. Only the air crew and maintenance staff for the planes were navy personnel. The actual ship's crew were merchant navy folk. At the end of the Second World War this composite vessel was converted into an oil tanker, returned to service and renamed *British Swordfish*. She was scrapped in 1959.

Fairfield's had a strong connection with Canadian Pacific but Harland and Wolff, too, built for the line. One particular ship was significant in several ways: *SS Minnedosa*. Her hull was actually built by Barclay Curle under subcontract to Harland and launched in Glasgow before being towed to Belfast for completion. This was a fairly unusual state of affairs as the Clyde yards tended to do their own thing. The 15,000-ton liner had an interesting life as well as an interesting construction history and in her early years was a regular, crossing the Atlantic out of Liverpool often carrying immigrants to Canada and America. In 1935 she was sold for scrap but bought by Mussolini's Italian government for use as a troop ship.

Ironically this made her a target for the Royal Navy and in particular the sub *HMS Umbra* which had a superb record for sinking Italian vessels in the Med. But *Minnedosa*, by now known as *Piemonte*, managed to survive a torpedo attack by *Umbra* and limped into Messina, but she was scuttled when Axis forces evacuated the port in 1943. The wreck was raised six years later and towed to La Spezia and scrapped. So ended another unusual life that had started on the Clyde.

Recently, warship building on the Clyde has concentrated on destroyers and frigates. The last major warship launched upriver was *HMS Ocean*, flagship of the Royal Navy. Known as "the Mighty O" she was an impressive sight off Campbeltown a few years ago during NATO exercises. She is not as awesome as the giant carriers of the US Navy but still eye-catching. Rather than being called a carrier she is more correctly an "amphibious assault ship" carrying large numbers of helicopters. Ray Bulloch, who had a long career in the yards and as a saturation diver in the North Sea oil fields, worked on her in the old Fairfield's, Govan, when it was under the ownership of Kvaerner, a Norwegian company.

He told me that there was a story around the Clyde yards and grog shops that she had been launched on a Friday the thirteenth and that was the cause of some launch bad luck causing extensive repair work to be done. An interesting yarn, but what today we would call an "alternative fact". Total rubbish. The launch date was 11 October 1995, which was not a Friday.

There is some amusing history here. As far as the British shipbuilding industry is concerned there has been an urban myth about bad luck and Friday launches for years. It dates as far back to the late 1880s when it is said the navy decided to dispel the stigma attached to a Friday launch by commissioning a ship called *HMS Friday*. The story goes that the keel was laid on a Friday and she was launched on a Friday, her maiden voyage began on a Friday the thirteenth under the command of Captain Friday. You will have guessed the end of this tale by now – she vanished and was never seen again!

Still heard often, the story is a complete myth. There has never been a navy vessel named Friday. But it makes for an interesting chat over a pint after a hard day in the yards. Shame to spoil a good story with the facts. Incidentally, one of *Ocean*'s predecessors *HMS Ark Royal* was relaunched after a major refit on Friday, 13 June in 2001. She successfully served another ten years at sea with not a problem!

10

Under Fire on a Seagoing Classroom in the Sun

Ask any Clydesider to name a German connection with the area and you will almost certainly get a response mentioning the deadly Luftwaffe bomber raids on Greenock and Clydebank – Second World War episodes that took a horrific toll of lives and burned memories unforgettably into the history of the area. But there is a rather surprising connection from the pre-war era now largely forgotten. It is gentler, more artistic, a different sort of history from that of bombers droning overhead and the darkness caressed by powerful searchlights piercing into the sky from defences on the banks of the river. Elsewhere in this book I mentioned cruising on the *Waverley* past its birthplace at A. & J. Inglis' yard, now completely swept away by the wrecker's ball. But in nearby Whiteinch there are two relics of the great days still standing which can be admired from the decks of the "last ocean-going paddler" in the world as the *Waverley* aficionados call the old vessel at every opportunity. One is the Titan crane built by Arrol upriver in the twenties and now a sadly rusting relic unlike the restored Titan in Clydebank. It is said the design of the Titan was the original model for one of the most popular Meccano toys. It is intriguing to think that some of those admiring what is left of Barclay Curle from the decks of the *Waverley* might have spent long winter evenings in the tenements of Glasgow, and the surrounding towns, carefully bolting together the tricky metal parts of the Meccano set they probably got as a Christmas present. The toy Titan took some building but it was worth it.

The other eye-catching object adjacent to the huge crane is the remains of one of the most interesting pieces of architecture in industrial Glasgow. The engine hall still has the name Barclay Curle built into the facade facing the river in an elegant and still modern-looking typeface. Next to the building in which the engines for the ships were built and then lifted into the hull by the Titan lie huge heaps of scrap iron waiting to be recycled. But even this proximity to mountains of ugly waste cannot obscure the class of the design of this industrial structure. It was built by John Galt but owes much to the ideas of the famous Modernist German architect Peter Behrens. Behrens was a remarkable figure in the history of architecture – Walter Gropius, Le Corbusier and Mies van der Rohe all worked in his office at some time – and he has similarities to the man considered by many to be Scotland's finest architect, Charles Rennie Mackintosh. Behrens was a member of the arts colony in Darmstadt in the early years of the last century. He was obsessively interested in all design matters, even designing his own typefaces.

Rennie Macintosh and his House for an Art Lover have strong Darmstadt connections. When in Darmstadt, Behrens built himself a house and, as Mackintosh would do with the design of the building that is now a tourist attraction in Bellahouston Park in Glasgow, he personally designed everything in it including the furniture, the towels, the pottery etc. The engine hall building still standing on Clydeside is a steel-framed brick and glass structure that was modelled on the design of the AEG turbine factory in Berlin. The gable ends were originally glazed, innovative and artistic for the time; there was a central isle with travelling cranes. It is typical of the style known as "industrial classicism". Eye-catching, the turbine hall is still today a significant touch of class in a scene of mostly industrial desolation. The yard itself was one of the earliest success stories of Clyde shipbuilding. It was started by Robert Barclay in 1818 in Stobcross moving to Whiteinch in 1876. By 1912 it was such a flourishing business that extra space was desirable and the Scotstoun yard of John Shearer & Sons was acquired. In the same year it was such an attractive proposition that the yard itself was bought by one of the legendary names in British Shipbuilding, Swan Hunter, a firm mainly based on Tyneside. It continued production at Whiteinch until 1968, churning out a succession of cargo/liners, tramp steamers and the occasional naval vessel. In the seventies Yarrow's bought part of the site and for a time the engine maker Sulzer worked there and, after the nationalisation of shipbuilding in 1977, Sea Dart and Sea Wolf missiles were manufactured on the site. Finally in the 1980s it became an industrial estate.

So ended the life of a famous Clyde yard, though it has to be said that Swan Hunter is more remembered for ships like the *Mauretania* which at one time held the Blue Riband for the fastest Atlantic crossing and the *Carpathia* which rescued some of the survivors of the *Titanic*'s infamous collision with that iceberg than anything from its Clyde associations. However, notable naval vessels produced in Whiteinch in the First World War were the curious "Insect" class gunboats. These were specialised, heavily armed shallow draught vessels designed for river work. In all, the navy had twelve of this class of gunboat and they saw service in the Mesopotamia campaign on the Euphrates and Tigris. They also saw action in Chinese waters and at home their armament made them suitable for anti-Zeppelin work. After the war several "Insect" class ships supported the White Russian anti-Bolshevik forces as part of an allied intervention in the Russian civil war. One vessel taking part in this adventure, the *Cicala*, wrote itself into history by taking part in a mutiny which was part of wider unrest in the Royal Navy at the time as a result of post-war austerity in the form of pay cuts. This mutiny was small compared to the Royal Navy mutiny in Invergordon, which is the subject of many books and is burned into the folk memory of Royal Navymen. After the Dvina incident, five seamen were sentenced to death for being ringleaders, but this was later reduced to five years' imprisonment.

After the Second World War, Whiteinch was notable for building a series of "City of" ships including the *Benares, Chester* and *Delhi*. Other eye-catchers for the riverside-enthusiast ship-spotters included the *Braemar Castle* and *Cawdor Castle*. But the two Barclay, Curle & Co. ships most remembered by Glasgow folk in particular are the *Nevasa* and *Uganda* both of which during their seagoing lives served for some years as educational cruise ships remembered with affection by thousands of West of Scotland kids who travelled and studied on them. An adventure on a "big ship" was a far cry from schoolwork in the grimy, industrial city itself. The *Nevasa*, launched in 1955 and scrapped in 1975, was built originally as a troopship for the British India Steam Navigation Company. The fact that it was a costly vessel to maintain contributed to its relatively short life. In 1966 passenger dress changed from grey flannels and sports jackets to white shirts and school blazers. Conversion work created fifty-two dormitories (named after famous naval figures like Beatty, Benbow and Nelson) and classrooms for the city children who set off south in excitable groups to the sun for cruising and an extra little polish to their education. The *Uganda* was a couple of years or so older and had been built as a cargo/liner, a sort of hybrid vessel popular before the era of the giant cruise liners. Its passenger capacity was 167, with 133 in tourist cabins, quite a contrast to the current stars of the cruise ship industry, which are floating resorts with around 4,000 passengers. On conversion to an education ship *Uganda* could accommodate 920 pupils. Both ships were much admired by connoisseurs for their elegant lines.

Uganda, in particular, had an adventurous life. In 1969 she was involved in a diplomatic incident in which fortunately no one was hurt. Cruising in the Atlantic off Cape Trafalgar, in international waters, she was fired on briefly by a Spanish shore battery, or so the papers said. Afterwards it emerged that since it was Trafalgar Day the skipper had decided to go inshore a bit for a better view of the Cape. The shore battery had been involved in a regular practice firing, said Spain. And the shells were blanks. None the less, Trafalgar Day or not, the *Uganda* put on speed and got out of the area fast! And in 1982 she was in a real war and on the front line. Converted to a hospital ship – call sign Mother Hen – she sailed to the Falklands. When she was "called up" she had been on a Med cruise and diverted to Naples to put ashore around 1,000 Scottish school kids. It was quite a sight for Italian journalists sent to the harbour to cover the story – they were met quayside by hordes of Scottish kids singing "Rule Britannia". She was refitted at Gibraltar with a helicopter pad, operating theatres and nursing wards. One hundred and thirty six medical staff, surgeons and nurses were taken on board and the exterior was painted white with huge red crosses on the sides. The *Uganda* played a valuable role taking wounded from the sinking destroyer HMS *Sheffield* and casualties from the land battle at Goose Green.

11

Bowler Hats, Battleships and Ballrooms

John Brown's is a contender for the title of the world's most famous shipyard. The names of the fighting ships it produced resonate to this day: *HMS Hood, HMS Tiger* and *HMS Repulse* from the early years and such as the battleships *HMS Duke of York, HMS Vanguard* and the aircraft carrier *HMS Indefatigable* from a later era. The list of ships built in this yard is a long one full of the names of memorable vessels like the *Lusitania* and *Aquitania,* and of course the famous Cunarders, *Queen Mary, Queen Elizabeth* and the *QE2.* A series of elegant liners were put together in the industrial landscape of the old town, ships whose grace and beauty when roaming the world were legendary. The wealthy elite who travelled in them dressed for dinner in the finest restaurants at sea and danced the tropical nights away in gilded ballrooms. A sharp contrast with the lives of their creators. The hard-working men who banged home the rivets and carefully crafted the state rooms, installed the plumbing and engineering, mostly lived in the Clydeside tenements that rose on both banks of the river often

When the *Lusitania* left Clydebank in 1906 few would predict that she would change history. But in 1915 she did just that. The Blue Riband holder, and for a spell the world's largest passenger ship, sailed from New York for a war zone and was torpedoed by a German U-Boat without warning off Ireland. Almost 2,000 died. Included in the total were many American citizens and the sinking appalled public opinion and hastened America's entry into the war.

Dramatisations such as this of the actual sinking of the great ship were effective. Germany tried to justify the sinking declaring they had treated the *Lusitania* as a naval vessel since they believed it was carrying munitions. The controversy went on for years. But in 1982 some British sources claimed there was a large amount of ammunition in the wreck.

In the years between the two world wars, HMS *Hood* was a symbol of British naval power "showing the flag" round the oceans of the world. But she was flawed by age and design failures and in 1941 in the Battle of the Denmark Strait she was sunk by German shells in an engagement with the battleship *Bismarck* and the cruiser *Prinz Eugen*. It was a massive blow to British morale as the public thought she was invincible.

It is hardly "flat pack" but the Clyde yards, particularly Denny and Yarrow's, once did good business exporting what were called knock downs – the completed vessels were taken apart and packed into crates for reassembly thousands of miles away. One such was iconic Mississippi stern wheeler the *Delta Queen*. After decades of service as an overnight river steamboat she was used as a hotel in Chattanooga before being restored and towed to Houma, Louisiana.

This is a replica of the *Comet* that in 1812 ran, on the Clyde, the first commercially successful steamboat service in Europe. Local shipyard apprentices built the replica in 1962 to mark the 150th anniversary of the first historic voyage and, on display in Port Glasgow, it makes the hard-working town worth a visit for anyone with an interest in maritime history. Only 45-feet long it was the start of something much larger – the legend of Clydebuilt.

Few of the famous Clyde puffers immortalised in Neil Munro's *Tales of Para Handy* still exist. For years these sturdy little vessels served remote west coast communities, often unloading on beaches. Originally they were steam-powered, but the Pibroch, one of the last, had a diesel engine and was built for the Islay distillery trade. In its final years it was a sad sight moored and decaying in Letterfrack, in Connemara, before being scrapped.

The most beautiful liner ever?
There is a long list of candidates
… among them the *Lusitania*, the
original Cunard Queens, *Mary* and
Elizabeth, the *SS France*, *SS United
States*, *SS Normandie* and *Canberra*.
My vote goes to the stunning QE2
and I suspect many of the "boat daft"
folk of Clydeside would agree. Here
head-on her style is eye-catching.
What a shame she is now laid up
and a sad sight in Port Rashid, Dubai.
ironically a place you'd think with the
money to save her.

without the benefit of even inside toilets. It is interesting to reflect that the majority of the men – with exception of the "bowler hats" and the well-paid in the drawing offices – who made these luxurious ships to transport the wealthy round the world never themselves travelled much further than the less glamorous Clyde holiday resorts. It is a dramatic demonstration of changing times that some of today's liners have more restaurants, bars and theatres than all the old seaside resorts put together.

The John Brown's story started upriver from modern Clydebank in Anderston in 1847. The men behind it, brothers James and George Thomson, who opened the Clyde Bank Foundry, had a good engineering pedigree. They had both worked for Robert Fulton. Four years after they had started their foundry they went on to open what they called the Clyde Bank Iron Shipyard at nearby Cessnock and quickly built up a good reputation for passenger ships. There was a hint of great days lying ahead when they build the SS *Jura* for Cunard. But it was not all easy success. Like many brothers, James and George had a falling out and split with George taking on the shipbuilding and James starting a new business. After their deaths the family who inherited the shipbuilding side were forced to move to new premises. The Clyde Navigation Trust threatened compulsory purchase of the yard as they wanted the land to build the new Prince's Dock. The Thomson solution was to build a new yard further down river at Barns O'Clyde. It was an ideal site across-river from where the River Cart entered the Clyde allowing the launch of huge ships. The Thomson foundry and engineering works were soon moved to the new site and one of the Thomsons became the First Provost of what was now known as Clydebank, a new town with housing for the workers in the engineering and shipbuilding industry. The name Barns O'Clyde slipped into history.

Down the years shipbuilding has been a turbulent industry with innovative new companies thriving and then failing and a seemingly constant turnover of owners and regular amalgamations in times of stormy financial waters. But Thomsons survived almost into the twentieth century despite some difficulties. In 1899 it was sold to a Sheffield steel makers called John Brown and Company. The price was around a million pounds, an enormous sum in today's currency. So began the great period of Brown's history from 1900 to the 1950s. Eventually competition from eastern Europe and the Far East led to a catastrophic decline in ship orders though latterly there was a brief flirtation with building oil rigs when the yard was owned by French company UIE. The Upper Clyde Shipbuilders consortium was formed in 1968 amid a perfect storm of financial difficulties and union disruptions. The hoped saviour of the Clyde collapsed after a mere three years in 1971. Brown's were only one of the victims.

Shipyard workers are known for their pawky sense of humour as well as a propensity for hard work and, on occasion, hard liquor. The tales of practical jokes played on apprentices are numerous and often recounted on stage by comedians who had worked in the yards. It was a hard, often dangerous place to earn your corn, and humour eased the days away and most of it, as remembered by the victims, was pretty harmless stuff – like that old one previously mentioned of sending a naive youngster to the stores for a dozen square circles or whatever. A favourite was for a foreman to ask an apprentice to go to the stores for "a long staund". On arrival the youngster was asked to wait in a corner for what indeed was a long stand. Other ploys were to send particularly hapless youths for a pot of tartan paint. Though my favourite was when a worker asked a fresh youngster to head over to the tool store for a new bubble for his spirit level adding "make sure it is the right size this time". The men themselves were great characters and old timers in riverside pubs will sup a fireside pint and tell tales of workmates. And not just the riveters, the joiners, the welders and the canteen workers; management, too, had its characters. And in the case of John Brown's no character stands taller than the truly legendary John Rannie who died in 1989 at the age of eighty-five.

In his days as managing director at Clydebank the yard bosses, as elsewhere on the Clyde, wore bowler hats. This was something of an "identifier". You may not have known the man wearing the hat, but if he was wearing a bowler you knew it might be wise to listen to what he had to say. The hat was also said by some to be the precursor of the safety helmet. Indeed if someone was to drop a nut or bolt onto my head I would rather wear a bowler than a fedora. John Rannie was more attached to his trademark headgear than most. Indeed in his *Glasgow Herald* obituary several Clydeside luminaries said they had never seen him outside without it. It seems he often told inquirers that he had bought it in Dunoon many years ago for what would be 50p. The more sanguine would suspect that he had many of the hard-wearing and stylish, for the day, hats.

John Rannie continued the tradition of the early owners, the Thomsons, in that he contributed much to the life of the town in addition to his work in Brown's. His involvement in the affairs of the place earned him the nickname "Mr Clydebank". He was proud to have been one of the few freemen of the burgh, receiving his burgess ticket in 1966. His obituary in *The Herald* contained a very human tribute from a man who could have been an opponent in the yards. Joe Brown, who was convenor of the shop stewards when John Rannie was managing director, told Scotland's premier broadsheet: "He was tough because it was that kind of industry, but I found him fair and compassionate. He was this way in his negotiations and also when dealing with promotions, where he tried objectively to analyse the capabilities of individuals." Mr Brown also praised John Rannie's forward thinking, remarking that he had been held back by the financial strictures surrounding the industry.

This view of John Rannie the man was part of a consensus. A fellow managing director, Ross Belch of Scott Lithgow, said he was "one of the great Clydeside shipbuilders". Fellow Clydebank man Alex Ferry, General Secretary of the Confederation of Shipbuilding and Engineering, said: "Everyone in the yard, from the chief naval architect to the youngest apprentice, knew who he was and respected him." And he had success further afield of the Clyde. In his early days he worked in Spain as a naval architect and on his retirement had a spell as general manager of a shipyard in Newfoundland. When he took up this job across the pond his new employers were losing a million Canadian dollars a year. When he left they were in the black. Some shipbuilder.

The ship mostly remembered in the John Rannie story is the *QE2* and in a later chapter the adventurous life of this elegant peacetime liner is told. It was just one of a long line of famous vessels to emerge from the yards. Many of the others wore the grey paint of the naval warship and were designed for more serious matters than making sure wealthy cruise passengers had a gin and tonic always to hand and entertainment and fine dining 24–7. Two of the most famous of these were the previously mentioned battle cruiser *HMS Repulse* and the battleship *HMS Hood*, both of which had sad ends with huge loss of life. Another much later battleship, *HMS Vanguard*, had a rather different distinction – she went to the scrapyard without ever firing a shot or facing an enemy in battle. The *Repulse* was the sister ship of *HMS Renown* also built on the Clyde, this time at Fairfield's, in 1916. When they went into service they were the fastest ships in the world with a top speed of almost 31 knots. Both warships had troubled births. Building them had been proposed before the outbreak of the First World War, but there were problems with the timescale and the design was revised. But towards the ends of their lives both warships played important roles in the Second World War, albeit in the end in different areas of conflict.

Like her sister, *Renown*, *Repulse* was eventually launched in 1916, not long after the battle of Jutland. In the final years of the Great War she served as part of the Grand Fleet in the North Sea. During this time she made a bit of aviation history when a Sopwith Pup, piloted by a Squadron Leader Rutland took off from a "flying off" platform constructed on top of one of the gun turrets. In the days before the demise of battleships and the emergence of giant aircraft carriers as the premier weapon of war, naval vessels were designed to allow a reconnaissance aircraft to be catapulted off such platforms and at the end of their mission they landed on the sea and were lifted back on board by a crane, if they were lucky. Today the sight of a powerful jet landing on the deck of a carrier pitching in heavy seas is awesome. There is no doubt about the bravery of the man at the controls. But the pilots of the biplane – "stringbags" – who flew from improvised platforms on converted warships were equally brave, or the layman might feel, even more mad than the jet jockeys. I remember a newspaper colleague who flew for the Fleet Air Arm telling me how scared he felt on a first solo flight at sea when he looked down from thousands of feet to his carrier, reduced to something like a speck on the ocean below. The realisation that he had to land his plane on that "moving speck" was a shock to the nervous system.

Pioneering aviation at sea apart, the *Repulse* also notably took part in what was known as "the battle of Heligoland Bight" in November 1917 in the closing months of the war. The crux of this old-time sea battle was efforts of the Royal Navy to prevent the Germans clearing paths for their warships through areas we had mined.

After the years of peace in the thirties the *Repulse* began operations as part of the Home Fleet's Battlecruiser Squadron in the North Sea on the outbreak of the Second World War and patrolled off the Norwegian coast in search of German warships. This was largely unsuccessful – in particular, a sortie to seek out six blockade runners that had broken out of Vigo in Spain. Another failure came in May 1941 when she was diverted from convoy guarding duty to try to find the *Bismarck*. Soon lack of fuel forced her to return to port. But spectacular action lay ahead, thousands of miles away in the Far East. After a refit that added to her armament, Winston Churchill, worried about Japanese aggression, decided to send a fleet including *Repulse* to Singapore. This was to be Force Z which included the battleship *Prince of Wales* and the carrier *HMS Indomitable* and some destroyers. On 9 December 1941 the force departed Singapore tasked with destroying Japanese troop convoys. The next day a Japanese submarine spotted the fleet, as did aircraft from enemy carriers. Realising their position was known the warships turned about, but despite manoeuvres to deceive the enemy another sub spotted them and fired five torpedoes which all missed. This was followed by eleven more planes hunting Force Z and several hours later an astonishing fleet of eighty-six bombers based in Saigon were launched carrying bombs or torpedoes. This was turning into a massive nautical battle. The first attacking wave dropped 500 lb bombs from around 11,000 feet.

The British ships hit back with anti-aircraft fire damaging

five of the Japanese bombers, and two were driven back to Saigon. But the Japanese were far from finished. *Repulse* was brilliantly handled by her captain, who managed to avoid nineteen torpedoes and some bombs. Eventually *Repulse* was then caught by a pincer attack involving seventeen torpedo bombers. Four or five torpedoes smashed into her causing fatal damage despite the warship's gunners shooting down two planes. *Repulse* capsized and 508 officers and men died. The survivors were rescued by escorting destroyers. So ended the life of one of the greatest of the warships built at Brown's. There was a sad, ignoble footnote to this spectacular naval battle when in October 2014, the *Daily Telegraph* reported that despite being designated war graves both *Prince of Wales* and *Repulse* were being "extensively damaged" with explosives by scrap metal dealers.

Perhaps the most famous of all the Brown's battleships was *HMS Hood*. This was a warship with a personal fascination for me. As I recounted in a previous book (*Scotland's Cruel Sea*), I first heard of it as a schoolboy. My dad and I shared a collection of pamphlets, postcards and books featuring the great ships built on the yards close to our home. Many a pre-TV era winter's night passed pleasantly browsing the books and hearing stories of folk who lived nearby and worked in the yards or served in the services. One pleasant wartime memory was of an uncle who flew bomber raids with the RAF and who on trips home brought me the unheard-of treat, in the days of rationing, of a Mars bar which it seems was often issued to air crew before going into action. Relatives in the navy never seemed to have been given such treats, though perhaps my dad got the occasional sip of navy rum. Amid grainy black-and-white shots of such famous ships as the *City of Paris*, the *Aquitania* and the Canadian Pacific Empress Liners one particular image fascinated me – *HMS Hood*, low in the water, ploughing through the Atlantic swells at high speed in an awesome flurry of spray. An immensely impressive sight. I didn't know it then, but the phrase "low in the water" played a big part in the story of the *Hood*. And her demise.

She was what navy men call a "wet ship" taking aboard tons of water in rough seas. Seawater would flow along her quarter decks and even get into mess decks and living quarters through ventilation shafts. Life on the navy's most noted and spectacular battleship was far removed from that of life on a liner. Indeed she was so "wet" she was often referred to by crew members as the biggest submarine in the navy. This was the result of poor design and botched alterations that left her vulnerable to plunging enemy shells. The loss of three warships in the Battle of Jutland in the years before the *Hood* was completed at Clydebank convinced the Admiralty that her design should be altered. Little wonder – the story is told that during the battle Admiral David Beatty, an aggressive, decisive and controversial commander, remarked to his fleet captain after two warships had blown up in half an hour: "there seems to be something wrong with our bloody ships today." Quite so, sir. Such sangfroid in action is perhaps not too surprising considering Beatty's gilded background. His wealth was largely based on a marriage to a woman who it is said at one time tried to cheer him up by saying that if he lost a warship she would buy him a replacement. Mind you, this was before Hitler started a shooting war and the Royal Navy was cruising the world "showing the flag" rather than chasing the new fast warships built by Germany in the interwar years.

Previously, Jutland battleships had heavy armour concentrated on the sides of the vessel leaving lighter armour for the decks. The reason for this was that most sea battles were then close range affairs with the trajectory of incoming shells close to the water line of the attacked vessel. Hence the concentration on protecting the sides of cruisers and battleships. But after Jutland the German high command had warships capable of throwing shells vast distances and then plunging down from great height on to the decks of their targets, often exploding in the areas where ammunition was held or removing power by direct hits on the engines. So towards the end of her build thousands of tons of extra deck armour was added at a cost to weight, speed and manoeuvrability to the *Hood*. All this resulted in the vessel, variously described both as "battleship" and "battle cruiser" going to war weighing far more than her original design. Known as the *Mighty Hood* and travelling at her top speed of more than 30 knots in heavy seas she certainly looked the part. But as often is the case, appearances can be deceptive. The *Hood* was more vulnerable than she looked. She was steaming to an inglorious end.

The *Hood* was supposed to be one of a fleet of four new ships whose design was based on experience in the First World War. They were intended to counter the threat of the German High Command's sleek and swift battle cruisers which were heavily armed. But in the world of warship design things were changing fast and the *Hood* was the only one of the four of the class to be built. One reason for the abandonment of the plan was the huge cost. Some at the top in the navy thought that the money would be better spent on merchant ships to replace those being sunk by the huge Nazi U-boat flotillas. There was great competition for resources by differing factions in the navy top brass. Maybe we should have been better to build submarines at the rate of the German naval yards.

At 800 feet the *Hood* was larger than the previous Renown class. Near enough 50,000 tons, her steam turbines could at one time push her along at a remarkable 32 knots. The US Navy was impressed and regarded her as extremely fast, more like a battle cruiser than a battleship. During her life, alterations and refits added weight and lowered speed, but she was still vulnerable to plunging shells despite the belated strengthening of the decks. She was launched in August 1918 by the widow of Rear Admiral Sir Horace Hood who was the grandson of Admiral Samuel Hood after whom the *Hood* was named. The flaws in her design, which were to be highlighted in the last great shooting wars of the battleship era, were of little importance in the 1930s.

In the years before the Second World War she cruised the oceans of the world displaying Britain's naval power. In those days, in the glossy resorts of the Mediterranean and elsewhere, the quality of the gin and tonics served to visiting politicians and important businessmen was of more concern than the strength of the steel plate used on the decks. The highlights of these years was a world cruise via the Panama Canal in 1923, but apart from the frequent visits to the sunshine of the Med there were cruises to Brazil and the West Indies. The United States, India, South Africa, Australia, New Zealand and Canada were also visited. No shots were fired from the great gun turrets, but there was one darker incident – on the way to the Med on yet another "showing the flag" cruise she was in collision with *HMS Renown*. The damage was minor though a huge dent in her flowing lines was not what the navy and the government wanted to show the world. There was also some damage to a propeller. This was not the image of competence she was intended to convey. And the court martials that followed were also bad news.

More serious times lay ahead. As the Second World War approached, it became apparent that the *Hood* was beginning to fail just at the time it was most needed. She needed time-consuming modernisation but more seriously the wear and tear brought on by the huge mileages of the gin and tonic days meant she now could not maintain her designed speed. She was forced to stagger on, used princi- pally in patrolling the areas around Iceland and the Faroes. The task was to protect convoys and intercept blockade runners trying to break out to the Atlantic. In one incident she was attacked by a Junkers Ju88 bomber and sustained damage that was repairable, but nonetheless added to her dire mechanical condition.

Next was a short spell in more southern waters before being sent to Rosyth along with *HMS Nelson* and *HMS Rodney* at a time when it was feared that the Nazis would attempt an invasion from the North Sea. When that threat receded it was time to go north to Scapa Flow in spring 1941. The end was closing in. Naval intelligence had indicated that the much feared *Bismarck*, the pride of the German Navy and a modern state-of-the-art warship superior in almost every way to the aging *Hood*, was heading out into the Atlantic. A group of ships including the *Hood* and *HMS Prince of Wales* was despatched to cut off the *Bismarck* and its companion, the equally dangerous *Prinz Eugen*, in the waters between Greenland and Iceland. A battle between these, the mightiest ships of the warring nations, began. It would not last long before the British suffered a shocking defeat.

Contemporary reports say the *Hood* spotted the Germans around dawn and opened fire on the *Prinz Eugen*. Both German ships immediately returned fire on the *Hood*. A shot from the *Prinz Eugen* swiftly hit the *Hood*. The salvo started a large fire. Minutes later when the British ship was on a sharp change of course in an attempt to position her guns she was hit again, this time by one of five salvos fired by the *Bismarck*. The British were being treated to a demonstration of superb gunnery by the Germans. This time a gigantic jet of flame leapt skywards from near the mainmast of the *Hood* and there was a huge explosion. Debris showered down on the fatally wounded ship. Astonishingly, some sources claim that she sank in just three minutes. However long it took, the fact is that 1,415 men died and only three sailors survived to be picked up by the destroyer *Electra*.

It was a devastating blow to British morale. The *Hood* had been an iconic symbol of the nation's naval power and in minutes it had been wiped from the face of the earth along with almost its complete crew. The news shook the nation. It was delivered to the folk back home and the wider world in an oddly worded communiqué from the Admiralty reading:

> British naval forces intercepted early this morning off the coast of Greenland German naval forces, including the battleship *Bismarck*. The enemy were attacked and during the ensuing action *HMS Hood* (Captain R Kerr, C.B.E R.N. wearing the flag of Vice Admiral L.F. Fleming) received an unlucky hit in the magazine and blew up. The *Bismarck* has received damage and the pursuit of the enemy continues. It is feared there will be few survivors from *HMS Hood*.

So shocking was the news to the navy at home that the message of its demise was decoded several times in the hope that it was some mistake. The *Mighty Hood* had been in the eyes of the man and woman in the street simply invincible. To suggest, as the authorities did, that the dreadful sinking was down to "a spot of bad luck old chap" is appalling. The cause of such a massive death toll and naval humiliation was much more complex than "unlucky" suggests. In addition to the *Hood* going down it is astonishing from this distance in time that the *Hood*'s companion *HMS Prince of*

Wales had to disengage the attack, despite managing to hit the *Bismarck* three times, because of mechanical failure in its turrets and guns. The *Bismarck* was repaired but later sunk. But that is another story or maybe a film!

Inquiries inevitably followed. The first, shortly after the sinking, concluded that the probable cause of the loss was "the penetration of one or more of the shells at a range of 16,500 yards, resulting in the explosion of one or more of the aft magazines." This hasty inquiry was criticised on several counts. One naval construction expert came up with the theory that the explosion of her own torpedoes had destroyed the ship. Another inquiry was held but it supported the findings of the first. Over the years there have been many other theories put forward. The wildest notion was that it was a malfunction of one of the ship's own guns that caused it to take in water so fast that the backbone of the ship broke causing it to plunge into the depths with the bows almost vertical. Diving expeditions in later years seem to confirm that the magazines did explode. It all seems rather academic now placed against the reality of the death toll.

The awesome sight of the huge bows of the *Hood* rising vertically before the final plunge was witnessed by one of the three survivors, Ted Briggs, who died in 2008. His testimony is moving. At the time that he lost his ship and his crewmates he was just eighteen and an officers' messenger. More than fifty years after the sinking, he said: "We had taken them by surprise and fired about half a dozen salvos before she replied. But when she did so her gunnery was excellent. The third salvo hit us at the base of the main mast which caused a fire. Then we were hit just above the compass platform which caused some bodies to fall down. I saw one officer with no face and no hands." Mr Briggs went on to say that he first saw the great ship as a boy of twelve and from that moment on he had wanted to serve on her. He wasn't alone in his admiration. The glamour of the early tours got massive newspaper coverage and the warship's pictures were splashed across the press. She projected power and prestige. But it was all to end in tragedy.

The end of the line of battleships built at Brown's came with the launch of *HMS Vanguard* in 1944. Her story is of significance to more than the history of the great ships of the Clyde – it was the end of the battleships worldwide. The days of huge warships with decks protected with thick steel plates and heavily armed with moveable gun turrets that could throw shells long distance from ship to ship, or to pound shore installations, had become history. The battleships were to be replaced in all the world's navies by smaller, faster and more agile missile-carrying destroyers and cruisers, aircraft carriers and submarines. An era was over and it ended in a whimper rather than one last glorious shoot-out on the high seas. For the *Vanguard* had a career conspicuous only for its lack of drama and it is said she never fired her mighty guns in anger. Instead she spent her seagoing years much in the style of the navy of the pre-war era, sometimes converted for use as glorified royal yacht and when not on such duties used as a figurehead of Britain's maritime might cruising the world showing the flag. She took part in endless exercises with friendly navies. But not fighting. There was barely an incident to talk about over gin and tonics in the wardroom before dinner. One rescue of a small merchant ship and a minor collision with an aircraft carrier was about as exciting as life got on *Vanguard*.

It was not meant to be this way. In the late 1930s and early 1940s, the Japanese and the Germans were in the lead in building battleships. Once again Britain was playing catch-up. Design work on a fast British battleship had begun in 1939 but building was a stop-and-start process as improvements identified as valuable, after experience when the Second World War started, were built into the new vessel causing delays and some frustration at Clydebank. In the end she was not commissioned until the war's end. At anchor at the Tail of the Bank she was an eye-catching sight. She had a rakish look with a flared bow and square-cut stern (the only one in the British Navy). She may not have been a fighter, but like a bronzed and muscled heavyweight boxer with a glass jaw she at least looked the part. She was expensive to run and of little use in the new era of maritime battles and her white elephant status was confirmed when she was sold for scrap and broken up in 1960. Good looks and the ability to take a crew of almost 2,000 for almost a thousand miles at a speed of 17 miles an hour was not enough to save her from the oxyacetylene cutters and she ended up being broken up back on the Clyde just a few miles downriver from her birthplace.

Even her final journey had a touch of farce. Being towed north from Portsmouth she slewed across the harbour and ran aground near a pub called the "Still & West". Five tugs eventually hauled her into deep water. The whole prolonged departure was watched in wry amusement by thousands who had gathered to wave her goodbye. That her graveyard was to be Faslane on the Gare Loch is ironic as the area was to become the home base for Britain's nuclear submarines including the next vessel to use the name *HMS Vanguard*, the nuclear-powered ballistic missile submarine. There was a final ironic touch – some of the steel salvaged from the scrapped battleship was later used as shielding in a nuclear laboratory.

12

The Blue Riband, Submarine Attack and Political Fury

The building of famous warships is, of course, only part of the illustrious history of John Brown's. For those with an interest in ships – including the men and women who built them – it is the glamour of the great liners that left Clydebank and sailed down the Firth of Clyde and out into the oceans of the world that are perhaps most remembered. The story of one in particular, the *Lusitania*, is still, more than 100 years after it sank off southern Ireland, a poignant mixture of seagoing triumph and tragedy. The triumph was being for a time the world's largest passenger ship and the holder of the Blue Riband as the fastest ship on the Atlantic. The tragedy was the death of almost 2,000 passengers and crew when the German submarine U-20 torpedoed her on 7 May 1915.

The Blue Riband was the most highly sought award in the world of shipping from around 1910 and was proudly claimed by ships of many nations. The name Blue Riband came from a term much used in horse racing. For ships it was an unofficial title of a competition with unwritten rules that meant that a liner with the speediest time for an eastbound Atlantic crossing could be called a "record breaker" but the real award only went to the fastest westbound crossing which was considered the more difficult since it went against the Gulf Stream. It is a demonstration of Britain's importance in world shipping that of the thirty-five liners to hold the record thirteen were Cunarders. Though, in an indication of what was to come in the current world of super cruise liners, the last holder of the famous old accolade was the stylish American liner *United States*. Indirectly the trophy was responsible for the construction of the *Lusitania* and her sister ship the *Mauretania* (built by Swan Hunter).

Cunard had been losing business to the fast ships of German companies Norddeutscher Lloyd (NDL) and the Hamburg America Line (HAPAG). The NDL liner *Kaiser Wilhelm der Grosse* had taken the Blue Riband from *Campania* and later HAPAG's *Deauchland* also claimed it, among other European liners. If Britain was again to rule the peacetime waves, new ships were needed and the first of the new flyers was to be built at Brown's. This work involved more than building a new ship. The whole of Brown's yard needed to be organised so that the ship could be launched diagonally across the Clyde where the river was at its widest, at the point the Cart joined it. The problem was that the ship was nearly 800 feet long and the river was only 610 feet wide. A new slipway taking up the space of two old ones had to be built. This was costly and almost £10,000 was spent on dredging the river. A further sum of almost £70,000, massive for those days, was spent on a new gas and electric plant, extending the dock and providing a huge new crane. This was far from a waste of money since, of course, it did more than allow the building of the *Lusitania* – it meant that for years ahead Brown's were well placed to bid for contracts to build some of the biggest ships of the day.

The *Lusitania* was launched on 7 June 1906. This was eight weeks later than planned because of strikes by the workforce. What's new? Six hundred invited guests watched and thousands of sightseers gathered at viewpoints round the yard. One thousand tons of drag chains were attached to the ship and six tugs were on hand. After sea trials, and early in service, it was clear that the demand for speed had been met. The new ship could transport more than 2,000 people at an average 25 knots (almost 30 miles per hour) and a one-day run at 32 miles per hour was achieved. Not bad for a 32,000 tonner more than 100 years ago. This was an engineering achievement. But in its interior design the *Lusitania* was also a success and a great favourite of Cunard passengers who were strictly segregated, as was the habit of the era – first, second and third class, spread over nine decks.

The first-class elite had the best of it of course. The first-class dining room was the most spectacular space in the ship taking space on two decks with the walls finished with mahogany panels. There was also the optimistic provision of a veranda cafe which might not have had much use considering the North Atlantic weather. For any toffs driven indoors there was the shelter of lavishly furnished and decorated reading and writing rooms, and a smoking room. All this is in sharp contrast to the accommodation of third-class passengers in the *Lusitania*'s forbearers. These ships often provided large open spaces where hundreds of people would share open berths with a few tables sometimes in the ad hoc sleeping quarters. *Lusitania*'s third class was designed to be much better than the norm. There was a ladies room and a smoking room that could be converted into dining rooms where passengers ate at long tables. And there was even a piano for their use. Instead of open berths there were two-, four-, six- and eight-berth cabins. The *Lusitania* was especially popular with immigrants. Mind you, those on the lower decks did not have the pleasure of the astonishing menus offered to the first class passengers. In a book on the last voyage of the *Lusitania* author Erik Larson reprints the menu for a typical meal. There are dozens of items, but the following list gives a flavour of the lavish dishes on offer:

> Oysters on the half shell
> Green turtle
> Fillet of sole au Gratin
> Boiled Codfish oyster sauce
> Ris de Veau Financière
> Hors d'oeuvres
> Potage St Germain
> Tournedos-Bernaise
> Cailles en Cocotte
> Braised Ox Tongue
> Haunch of Mutton
> Boiled Capon
> Sirloin and Rib of Beef
> Cauliflower
> Spinach
> Boiled rice
> Potatoes boiled, Garfield or mashed
> Roast Mallard Duck-hominy fritters
> Salad
> Saxon Pudding
> Tartlets Viennese
> Plum tart
> Bavarois Rubanné
> Vanilla and strawberry ice cream
> Tea and coffee

From the grill (15 minutes) spring chicken,
sirloin steaks, mutton chops

To wash your selection down there was a wine list thick with the finest vintages, expensive brandies and a selection of whiskies and liquors as extensive as any to be found in the finest restaurants in Paris or London.

Passengers on Atlantic crossings – the *Lusitania* made more than 200 – were a pampered lot if they could afford top fares. Cunard liked to do things in style and I would guess that meals served to VIPs and others on the sea trials off Arran in the summer of 1907 would not have been sandwiches and tea. But if the catering was fine, the result of the trials were not. Speed was not a problem as the massive power produced by the turbines running at 194 revolutions a minute produced 76,000 shaft horse power. Test runs were made on the "measured mile" off Arran and on runs off Cornwall. Speed tests were also conducted between Arran and Ailsa Craig and the Isle of Man. The contract speeds were easily reached. But at a cost. Down the years the main problem for fast liners was that enemy of comfort – vibration. It was so troublesome on these early "shake down" *Lusitania* cruises that the stern second-class accommodation was unusable.

To fix it required a rebuild and strengthening of large areas at the stern of the ship. Part of the problem was caused by the design of the giant four propellers. Initial fixes were enough to allow the ship to go into service but vibration dogged her all her life. After a couple of years the propellers were changed and the alterations created a small increase in speed and reduced the vibration.

Looking back from the days of supersonic aircraft, international space stations and super jumbo passenger planes, it is hard to appreciate the public appetite for following the fortunes of the great liners. But facts speak for themselves – *Lusitania's* maiden voyage for example gathered 200,000 people to see her leave Liverpool. Despite her engines not being fully run in and running into some fog she reached New York in five days and fifty-four minutes, only thirty minutes slower than the then Blue Riband holder, *Kaiser Wilhelm II*. In the States it is said hundreds of thousands in Battery Park watched her sail up the Hudson to New York's legendary Pier 56.

New York police cancelled all holidays and the cops were out in force to control the crowds. On the quayside 100 horse-drawn cabs waited in line to take the wealthy passengers to their fancy hotels up town. It was a magnificent sight for lovers of ships and horses! During her first stay in the Big Apple the ship was open to guided tours and New Yorkers were shown what the latest in luxury at sea was like. The *Lusitania* was a favourite with the American elite and her close association with New York was cemented when she featured in 1909 in the Hudson-Fulton Celebration which marked the 300th anniversary of Henry Hudson's trip upriver and the 100th anniversary of Robert Fulton's steamboat *Clermont*. As part of the fun Wilbur Wright brought his Wright Flyer to the city. Most New Yorkers had never seen a plane and gaped in awe as it flew directly over the moored *Lusitania*. Few would have thought that the fragile wooden and canvas contraption soaring over their heads would lead to giant jets and the end of transatlantic liners.

The great ship herself was not to live to see the arrival of jetliners. Her demise in 1915 was one of the major incidents in the First World War and caused diplomatic uproar and shocked Britain and America. Until she left New York on May Day 1915 her Atlantic crossings had gone largely without incident. But anyone leaving on her for Europe at war should not really have been surprised at the tragic end of the voyage. That the seas around Britain had been declared a war zone by Germany, which had a large and efficient fleet of submarines, was well known. And in America the German embassy had even taken newspaper adverts warning of the danger of travelling on the *Lusitania*. Passengers who spent the crossing in an unworried state of mind must have dipped too deeply into that wine list mentioned earlier. Clearly the danger increased with every mile steamed nearer to Britain. The end came without warning a mere eleven miles off the coast of Ireland.

As everyday life continued on board the luxury liner, and home came into sight, it was a different scene underwater. Nearby U-20 was patrolling in search of targets under the command of Kapitänleutnant Walther Schwieger, one of the great U-boat aces of the First World War. Schwieger sank more than 200,000 tons of shipping. And killed more than 2,000 people. But as he manoeuvred to place the unsuspecting liner into the cross hairs of his attack periscope he was probably unaware of just what the effect of sinking one ship would have on the war. (However, it was later said that he had identified it as the *Lusitania* from the four funnels and the size of its masts.) Around 1.40 p.m., as waiters scurried about on the luncheon service, he had spotted the target. Finally he unleashed a single torpedo (some accounts contest this) from less than 1,000 yards range and hit the target on the starboard side below the bridge. The initial explosion was followed shortly by another unexplained internal explosion. One of John Brown's finest took a mere eighteen minutes to sink. One thousand one hundred and twenty-eight people lost their lives. After the war a fascinating fact emerged. Apparently fifteen minutes after he had fired his torpedo, Schwieger noted in his war diary:

It looks as if the ship will stay afloat only for a very short time. [I gave order to] dive to 82 ft. and leave the area seawards. I couldn't have fired another torpedo into this mass of humans desperately trying to save themselves.

The sinking started immediate controversy and diplomatic wars. The Germans had sunk an officially non-military passenger ship without warning which appeared to be a breach of internationally agreed rules of war. And on the face of it that seems clear. But it was much more complex, for the British themselves had made it impossible for subs to warn crews to abandon ship before they fired when they started using what were known as Q-ships. These were armed vessels disguised as commercial ships, who only revealed their guns when attacked. Interestingly there is little dispute that the *Lusitania* had been fitted with gun mounts in 1913 before the start of the war, but she was unarmed on the final voyage.

Germany justified thinking of the *Lusitania* as a naval ship and a legitimate target because she was suspected of carrying hundreds of tons of war munitions. (Was this the cause of the second explosion? No one really knows.) Their politicians and high command also claimed that the attack was legal since Britain was said to have breached the rules on which ships carried what since the start of the war. A further complication in the diplomatic furore was that around 130 American citizens had died. There is little doubt that this had a huge effect on anti-German public opinion in the States and that it helped push America into the war, though this did not happen for a couple of years. After the end of the war the British government continued to insist year after year that there were no munitions on board. But in 1982 the head of the Foreign Office's North

America department admitted there was a large amount of ammunition in the wreck lying 300 feet down. War and politics can be a dirty game.

The *Aquitania*, along with the *Mauretania* and the *Lusitania*, is another of Cunard's early four-funnelled liners to stay strong in maritime memories. The expensive new plot where the *Lusitania* was built was showing its worth. The keel of the *Aquitania* was laid in the same ground which was later used to construct the *Queen Mary, Queen Elizabeth* and *QE2*. The sinking of the *Titanic* had focused public attention on safety at sea and the *Aquitania* was one of the first of the new huge liners to carry what seems now so obvious – lifeboats capable of taking all passengers and crew to safety in the event of a disaster. This meant that in future the lifeboats on both port and starboard sides could evacuate all on board even if the stricken vessel had one side under water. Eighty lifeboats (two were motorised and had wireless equipment) were carried. *Aquitania* is often referred to in the archives and newspaper articles as "the ship beautiful" and looked particularly fine when painted white as a Red Cross ship in the First World War. Beauty apart, she has a place in history as she survived in service of one kind or another for thirty-six years, a record among the great liners. She was converted to military use in both world wars and survived to go back into service after both. Eventually maintenance and fuel costs caught up with her and she was a sad sight in her final years before she was scrapped at Faslane in 1950. At least she died close to her Clydebank birthplace.

13

Trouble on the Drawing Board
and Financial Storms

Those early Cunarders had undoubtedly beautiful lines but today they look like ships sailing across the dusty pages of maritime history. Apart from the *Lusitania* John Brown's built another top contender for the most beautiful liner ever – the *QE2*. Even in retirement its lines have a classic modern look. Today shipping lines like Royal Caribbean, with vessels such as its gigantic *Oasis of the Seas*, take a huge slice of the growing cruise market. But even as a cruise aficionado I have to admit that these vessels, and others of similar appearance from Princess Lines, Carnival and NCL etc. do not lift the heart of a ship lover as they roam the world. One veteran of the Clydeside yards looking at such a vessel, docked at Greenock, a port which is now attracting a growing number of cruise ships, remarked to me that it looked like a tower block that had toppled over on its side into the sea and somehow managed to float. I could not disagree. So it is heartening that Cunard at least has managed to retain something of the old style in its modern replacements for the old *Queen Elizabeth*, *Queen Mary* and

QE2 (*QM2*, *Queen Elizabeth* and *Queen Victoria*). Sadly these new ships were built in France (Chantiers de l'Atlantique) and Germany (Blohm + Voss) rather than on the Clyde, but at least they still feature the traditional red and black outside livery and vintage style sterns, some evidence that their designers have not completely capitulated to the money men's demands for more and more cabins at the expense of external elegance. In Southampton, New York, Fort Lauderdale, and ports like Venice and Athens on the Mediterranean cruise circuit, these Cunarders still have something of the appearance of real seagoing ships. They stand out as a bit different among the serried ranks of floating blocks of flats.

Perhaps some of this is due to Cunard's heritage as the earlier Queens, designed before the jet age stole the trans-atlantic market, were primarily ferries, albeit gigantic fast ferries, rather than floating holiday resorts. Interestingly, unlike most of its competitors the *QM2* recently, for part of the year, filled this limited role with speedy crossings from Southampton to New York. Modern cruise liners generally cruise at around 20 knots – the original Queens and the legendary *France* could routinely hit 30 knots. An illustration of the remarkable speed of the great liners is the fact that the *United States* in 1952 made a passage of almost 3,000 miles from the Ambrose Light in Lower New York Bay to Bishop Rock, a few miles off the Scilly Isles, at an astonishing average speed of almost 36 knots, almost double the cruising speed of today's floating resorts. In the days when great ships routinely tried to win the Blue Riband for the fastest crossing, speeds above 30 knots were commonplace. Now only the *QM2* can boast of anywhere near such a top speed. These days most of the cruise liners spend the day tied up in dock and passages are made at night allowing passengers to wake up to a new port and new scenery every day. I found this a bit irksome on a recent journey as I had looked forward to passing through the Dardanelles and seeing the battlefields of the First World War and then the straits of Messina and a look at the progress on the controversial troubled bridge between Sicily and Calabria, which if ever finished will be the world's longest suspension bridge. Disappointingly, it was dark with nothing to see.

The question of which was the most beautiful of the great liners will always cause some argument but few would dispute that for many years the *QE2* was the most recognisable ship to sail the world. Her yard number in Brown's was 736 and the keel plates were laid on 2 July 1965, in the same berth where the old *Queen Elizabeth* and *Queen Mary* had been built. But before work started there had been years of debate on the design of the new liner. World shipping, freight and passenger, was in a period of change. Everyone in Cunard seemed to have different ideas of what the new ship should look like and what facilities it should have. Initially the successor to the Queens was to be dedicated to the Atlantic service (and not suitable for cruising) which at the time was still profitable and the fact that the big jets would kill that trade was not properly appreciated. Had this ship, codenamed *Q3*, been built it would have been a disaster for Cunard since unlike the *QE2* it would have been too large to reach most of the popular cruise ports. Gradually the theory that the new vessel should be dual purpose, transatlantic service and cruising, began to take hold. And the proponents of this concept eventually won the day. But tradition was still a factor in these different times. An example of what was deemed important was that amid all the meetings on specifications for the engines needed and decisions like the number of lifeboats, and where they should be placed, time was found to discuss the weighty matter of quarters for the passengers' servants. But, at least, these meetings recognised the changing world and it was pointed out that in 1963 the old *Queen Elizabeth* carried forty-two servants at special rates. Other issues like the number of dog kennels were also downgraded in importance.

Several blind alleys were traversed before the design was finalised. But after years of work the design was agreed and documents spelling out what was required were made ready for the yards who would be asked to tender. Even this, far from the final detailed plans, was an impressive enterprise – the hull specification alone amounted to more than 200 pages of closely typed information and the specification details of the machinery and electrical requirements took more than 300 pages. This was time-consuming and tedious work in the days before computer aided design and on-screen simulations had really begun to revolutionise shipbuilding, though when actual construction work began in the yards computers were beginning to play a major role particularly in keeping track of materials and fabrication progress. Five yards were asked to tender on the basis of these early documents. But Cammell Laird of Birkenhead and Fairfield's quickly announced they would not be tendering. This left John Brown's, Harland and Wolff and a consortium involving Swan Hunter and Wigham Richardson and Vickers Armstrong.

When the tender documents hit the boardroom table in Liverpool there was a considerable shock for Cunard. They had based all the financial calculations on the new vessel on a cost of around £22m. The would-be builders found this optimistic and also those offering the lowest price would not tender on a fixed-price basis. All sorts of alterations would have to be made to the plans to get near the desired price and timetable and as a result ideas for expensive new innovative luxuries were ruthlessly slashed out. Other savings were found like eliminating one boiler and dropping plans for an aft cargo hatch. But blue pencils were kept sharpened and busy crossing out all sorts of things thought non-vital. The dream of what the new ship might be like was being watered down. The plans were examined in such detail that a million pounds could be cut off the price by such a raft of seemingly small savings. Class consciousness did seem to come into play when it was decided what was to go and what was to stay. The crew lost washbasins in their cabins and the toffs in first class had to store expensive coats in stateroom wardrobes rather than a special "fur store"! Eventually a price of £24.5 million, subject to escalation of wage rates and the price of materials, was agreed, with Brown's winning the contract. The raising of the money was an incredibly complex financial project and to help pay for the new ship Cunard had mortgaged some of its other ships and borrowed heavily from a consortium of banks. The government provided aid in the shape of a loan to make sure that a new British showpiece could be built. The signing of the contract, with a delivery date of May 1968, took place in the Bank of England. The final cost was around £30m, an equivalent of £500m at today's rates.

Cunard had cast off on an awesomely risky financial voyage. *The London Times* summed it up thus: "What Cunard has embarked on is a unique compromise between express liner and cruise ship. No one has attempted it before (the existing big ships on the Atlantic, the Queens and the *France* and the *United States*, were driven to cruising by falling winter traffic; they were not designed for it). It remains to be seen if the two are commercially reconcilable. Everything depends on the Atlantic traffic in volume and revenue holding up enough to keep her busy for about seven months each year. Ship owners are accustomed to speak of acts of faith and courage. The country will applaud both owners and builder and wish them well."

And there would be no more fervent well wishers than those on Clydeside who had experienced the dark days when work on the old *Queen Mary* had been halted in 1931 by the Great Depression. The memory of that partly finished hull towering for years over the streets of Clydebank where thousands looked for work was not easily forgotten. The great ship is now an affectionate memory for most people and early problems and disappointments, and there were many, are often forgotten. Maybe there was a hint of what was to come in the fact that even the keel laying did not go quite to plan. The ship was to be laid down on the same piece of ground in the yards used for the old Queens and other legendary Clydebuilt liners like the *Lusitania* and the *Aquitania*. It was to take place on 2 July 1965 watched by assorted Cunard bigwigs full of optimism. Speeches were made and toasts drunk. But embarrassingly the first sections of the keel could not be moved into place that day because of unforeseen technical problems – despite a dummy run the previous day – and in fact the keel was not properly laid until the day following the planned event.

The final statistics of the new ship are an indication of just what a massive construction undertaking it was – length 963 feet, beam 105 feet, draught 32 feet 6 inches, tonnage 65,000. Double reduction-geared turbines powered twin screws. The relative narrowness of the ship is a result of building it to be able to traverse the Panama Canal. It was the maximum size possible for this task and such ships were known in the trade as "Panamax". In fact there are only a couple of inches or so on either side of such a vessel when in one of the giant locks. This brought an amusing conversation I was told about by a veteran Clydebank

116

man. Apparently he met, in a bar no doubt, a fellow Scot who was a pilot on the canal. "Are you no worried about scraping it on the lock walls?" asked the local. The pilot's typically Clydeside laconic reply was that it didn't worry him as it was "no my ship"!

Like today's floating resorts which it preceded, the *QE2* towered high over the water. There were thirteen decks, four swimming pools, restaurants and entertainment spaces galore. Passenger capacity was 2,025 and officers and crew 906. But all the swithering over the final design and the cost-saving alterations were knocking the project off its projected timescale. John Brown told the owners in 1966 that the new ship could not be delivered on time meaning that profit targets from the North Atlantic summer season would be lost. A factor in all this was out of the control of Brown's – a long seamen's strike cost Cunard dearly. Mind you, the delays allowed the ship's designers and the yard's craftsmen extra time to fine-tune the specification.

Even to this day most people's memory of the *QE2* is of its funnel, so different from the undistinguished smoke stacks on the two great Queens that preceded her. The design of this new funnel was both practical and aesthetic. The old-style funnels were always a source of problems with smoke and exhaust gases blowing down on the decks in certain conditions. The new design came after wind tunnel tests of twenty different designs. The chosen design had wind scoops round the actual smokestack to sweep exhaust gases and smoke upwards away from the passenger deck. In addition, this solution to an old problem gave the new vessel a sort of unique grace much admired in connoisseurs of liners. (However during a major refit in the late eighties which involved a switch in power from steam power to diesel electric the funnel had to be altered to accommodate new exhaust pipes for the German engines.)

In the newspaper game in Glasgow at the time, I well remember the growing excitement as the ship grew great in the yards, her hull easily seen in gaps in the tenement houses that lined the streets of Clydebank and from the fields and roads across the river. Regular progress reports in the morning and evening papers kept readers in the loop as they say these days. The planned coverage of the launching dominated newspaper executives' thoughts for months. Supplements featuring "exploded cutaway" drawings of the new super ship were planned and picture editors searched for the best points to capture the moment the giant first floated. Clyde launches were traditionally high days in the yards. The official party, the great and good, would sip champagne and nibble lobsters, but in the pubs and working men's clubs there were also celebrations though of less ostentation. This launch however was the most important for years. British shipping had been on a downward curve for years and this was to be the beginning of a new era of prosperity for the Clyde in particular. In retrospect it didn't quite work out that way. There were few great liners or indeed cruise ships to follow. The slow decline in the tonnage produced and the change to concentrate on building tankers, container ships and warships was a growing shadow in the background of this great day. But it didn't spoil the fun for the thousands who watched, for the workers and their families, for the press who turned up mob-handed, for the growing army of TV cameramen. This was a day making history.

The scheduled time for the launch was 2.30 p.m. But two minutes before the appointed time Queen Elizabeth moved across the launching platform and using the traditional form of words said, "I name this ship Queen Elizabeth the Second. May God bless her and all who sail in her." This ended the speculation of months on what the name of the

118

new Cunarder would be. But it contained something of a shock for insiders. In their authorised history of the ship Neil Potter and Jack Frost say: "We can reveal that this was a last-minute change of name by the Queen herself; and by 'last minute' we mean a mere matter of seconds before she launched the liner. Four people knew the name of the liner, agreed by the Queen, was simply Queen Elizabeth. But seconds before the launching the Queen suddenly decided in her own mind that the ship should be called Queen Elizabeth the Second and so she gave it that name." Some dispute this version of how the name came about, but to me the Potter/Frost account rings true.

Most were happy at the change. But not the then much less politically significant Scottish National Party. They took it as an insult since they had never recognised the Tudor Queen Elizabeth as a Scottish royal. The familiar old red post boxes at the end of every second or third street with Queen Elizabeth II on them were like a red rag to a bull to the Nats. The name of the new liner stirred even more fury. Even those astute observers of society, the bookies, had given odds of fourteen to one on the words "the second" being used. However, one man who was happy was the legendary Managing Director of Brown's, John Rannie, he of the bowler hat, who was quoted as saying: "She is a Queen and I like the name." The ship had an adventurous life in wartime and peace and was never far out of the headlines. In particular there were umpteen early breakdowns involving the steam turbines that for a while tarnished the reputation of the ship.

Whatever the nasty newspaper comment there was about the teething trouble, particularly in the technical press, there was one area where there was nary a word of criticism – the internal design and decoration.

After teething problems and delays the maiden voyage

from Southampton to New York began on 2 May 1969 – and for the record it took four days sixteen hours and thirty-five minutes. The first civilian passenger had been Prince Charles who had been on board along with William Warwick, her first skipper, when she moved from the Clydebank yard to Greenock for finishing work in dock. Just a couple of years later the first of many adventures took place when she helped rescue 500 passengers from a burning French ship. Not long after this there was the drama of a bomb threat on a sailing to New York. This would have made a wonderful episode in a cinematic biography as a combined Special Air Service and Special Boat Service team parachuted into the sea alongside the liner and then boarded it to search for the "bomb". No bomb was found but a hoaxer was collared by the FBI.

These rather minor dramas, and the technical problems, were largely forgotten in 1982 when the QE2 became something of a war hero in the turbulent times of the Falklands conflict. The early designers had succeeded in giving the ship the aura of a super-size super yacht unlike most of her modern competitors who were more like floating tower blocks as has been mentioned. But this giant "super yacht" went to war in the service of her country. In its new guise it was certainly no gigantic gin palace and resort, but a vital weapon of war.

Before she headed to the South Atlantic a great deal of work had to be done to convert her to a military transport and hospital ship. It was not much more than a month after the Argentinians had invaded the islands when in May 1982 the interior luxury of the ship, requisitioned by the Admiralty, was torn apart and major alterations made. The job in hand was to take thousands of troops to the front line in the battle to free the Falklands. In civilian life one of the most pleasant memories of a voyage in the QE2 was gliding across acres of opulent carpets so thick that it was like having a new comfy spring in your step. The refit took place in Southampton and one of the first actions was to cover those valuable and beautiful carpets with common old hardboard. One glance at this former luxury now a muddy brown colour and you knew that the war game was for real. Boots designed to yomp around the rough terrain of the Falklands were not to be allowed to damage the carpets.

Anyone used to the pleasures of a well-furnished state-room or suite would have gasped at how public lounges had been turned into basic dormitories for the squaddies. But all this was cosmetic. More vital changes were made to the structure. Helicopter pads were more important than swimming pools and two were added. Huge ugly piping was installed in order to allow fuel to get to the engine room when refuelling at sea. The huge ship was vulnerable to air attack and mines and to combat the latter an anti-magnetic device was fitted around the hull. In addition, much of the hull was strengthened with new steel plating. Gradually a thing of beauty became much more utilitarian. It is remarkable that the transformation only took a couple of weeks. The "passengers" were 3,000 soldiers and included battalions of the Gurkhas, Welsh and Scots guards and members of the Blues and Royals booked for travel to South Georgia. Six hundred and fifty Cunard crew members sailed with them to look after their needs with regard to food, watering and sleeping arrangements. On the food front the fare was pretty regular stuff though there was the occasional taste of smoked salmon. And there was waiter service by experts in the trade, not something you expect in a services canteen. The QE2 was part of a remarkable task force – forty-three Royal Navy ships, twenty-two from the Royal Fleet Auxiliary and sixty-two merchant ships.

For the soldiers this was no freebie, they knew they were heading into danger. The entertainment on board this unique voyage seemed, on the account of those who returned, to largely consist of massive card sessions where quite a bit of cash changed hand. But most of the time training was conducted out on the decks. In the days when rubbish bags were routinely cast overboard they were filled and used for makeshift target practice. Early rises were obligatory, mealtimes staggered (though officers still got to take theirs in the old first-class grill rooms) and battalions took turns to run round the decks.

The voyage was hugely risky and made under conditions rarely if ever experienced by a liner – the ship was blackened out against air attack, the radar switched off, and she steamed on without many modern navigation aids. But she made it safely to Cumberland Bay, South Georgia, and army men transferred onward nearer the front line by P&O's *Canberra* since the *QE2* was too vulnerable to attack to go too close to the conflict. Despite the successes of the war the voyage home was sombre. A super-size super yacht was now a giant floating hospital. Six hundred survivors of the sinking of the Royal Navy ships *Ardent*, *Antelope* and *Coventry* were on board. And medics and the Cunard volunteers had to deal with heart-breaking injuries. The return to Southampton water in June 1982 was an emotional affair. The Queen Mother was aboard the Royal Yacht *Britannia* and in response to her greeting, Captain Peter Jackson signalled: "Please convey to Her Majesty Queen Elizabeth our thanks for her kind message. Cunard's *Queen Elizabeth 2* is proud to have been of service to Her Majesty's Forces". For the great ship and the crew who sailed in her to the drama of the Falklands, it was back to the old routine. The ship had barely docked when workers swarmed aboard and conversion back to her old luxury started.

The Falklands campaign was no doubt the most exciting period in the life of this ship, but there were many other adventures along the way. It was an eventful life with many ups and downs – not at all surprising considering she sailed almost six million miles in sunshine and storm (including 806 Atlantic crossings) and carried around 2.5 million passengers in the process. Not long after the refurbishment and annual overhaul in autumn 1983 a cruise had to be cancelled because of boiler problems. Almost a year later an electrical fire caused complete loss of power delaying scheduled sailings for several days. All this led to a rethink by the owners and a decision was taken to convert to diesel power. New propellers were also fitted and passenger accommodation refurbished. The hope was that this would give her another twenty years of profitable life.

Some years later in 1992 there was a less routine happening. Returning from a cruise to Halifax, Nova Scotia, along the east coast of the United States there was an old-fashioned accident, surprising in these days of radar and highly detailed modern charts. She ran aground close to Cuttyhunk Island near Martha's Vineyard, severely damaging the hull, though all the passengers suffered was inconvenience. Part of the problem was that while travelling at top speed the hull began to "squat" down, increasing her depth in the water. This affected her draft and took her on to an apparently uncharted shoal with her hull scraping rocks in the shallow water. Later, divers found red paint on the rocks – it had been a fairly violent collision between ship and land. The passengers lost several days' cruising on their expensive holiday and ended up decanted in Newport Rhode Island. The liner was taken to Boston for temporary repairs in a suitable dry dock.

A few years after this the Cunard board decided that

another makeover was needed. In a hint of what was to become in the future the norm for Cunarders, the multimillion-pound project was given to a German yard. After the refit, the liner had a bit of a fright in 1995 when she encountered a rogue wave 200 miles south of Newfoundland thought to be an awesome 90-feet-high wave caused by a hurricane. A drama, but she survived, and as the nineties drew to a close and she celebrated the thirtieth anniversary of her maiden voyage, one of the longest farewell tours in history was about to begin. Cunard had been bought by Carnival Corporation in 1999 and the ship given yet another makeover, this time at a cost of $30 million. Much of this cash was spent on the various public rooms which were showing their age badly. There was also redecoration for the passenger cabins and the old style upmarket shops replaced by the typical perfume boutiques and expensive watch outlets of the sort so beloved by the modern cruising fraternity. But the exterior was not ignored and the hull stripped and repainted in the traditional Cunard colours. It was a badly needed injection of modernity but did nothing to slow the inevitable decline and the day when she would permanently be moored in some foreign harbour, if not torn to bits by the wrecker's ball.

In 2004 the transatlantic sailing became a memory and cruising was the full-time job. Though still among the fastest afloat, at 28.5 knots, this was in fact a disadvantage. Cruising is at its best as a money maker for owners when your ships spend days quietly in harbour and nights pottering along at around 20 knots or less heading towards the next "must see" destination and thereby saving greatly on fuel. And maximising the onboard spend. During her later years, in 2005, there was an unsavoury incident when crew members, drunk from a private party, went on the rampage vandalising valuable artwork. The ship had always been something of a floating art gallery, indeed for the wealthy this had been one of her attractions. On this occasion a tapestry commissioned for the launch was thrown overboard, a portrait of the Queen damaged, as was the entertainment area, and in addition a lifeboat was damaged. Not surprisingly, sackings followed but it could have been worse. Indeed it would take pages to list all the works of art that sailed the world with the *QE2*. A flavour of what was on view can be conveyed by the fact that the on-board collections included a solid silver model of the ship made by Asprey of New Bond Street, London, a set of antique Japanese armour and a Wedgwood vase presented to the ship by Lord Wedgwood. The corridors and public rooms were adorned by hundreds of paintings by celebrated artists. Modern cruisers are often compared to floating hotels. The *QE2* could have been called a floating museum. Over the years all sorts of artistic artefacts were collected along the way adding to the displays.

Some will tell you that all great political careers end in tears and perhaps the same could be said of great ships. Certainly the *QE2* did not go quietly to a safe and secure retirement home where she could rest up in peace and enjoy the respect she deserved. Instead there were years of uncertainty and so far no satisfactory conclusion as to what was to happen to her. Interestingly the original Cunard Queens likewise had far from happy retirements. But the *QE2*'s demise was influenced by a number of factors other than the fact that her design was not a good economic model in the twenty-first century. In 2007 she was sold to the Dubai investment company Istithmar for $100 million. The decision a year later to take her out of commission was partly forced on the owners. New safety regulations to be introduced in 2010 by the International Convention for the Safety of Life at Sea meant that major and highly expensive changes would have had to be made to her superstructure. The end was in sight, but there were some voyages still ahead before the hawsers were thrown ashore for the last time. Most poignant of all was a farewell tour of the British Isles that brought out "boat daft" families in their millions. For those who had travelled on her and worked on her, for those who had always wanted to do either, and for those who built her, this was a chance for a final memory of seagoing glory. Every mile of this last voyage was watched from the shore by thousands and followed by television cameras and legions of newspaper feature writers and snappers – a great icon of Britain's maritime history was "sailing by" for the last time. Tears, cheers and smiles mixed in an emotional farewell.

The farewell cruise began in Cork on 3 October 2008, and she headed towards Douglas Bay on the Isle of Man and on to Liverpool. The next stop was Belfast and then Greenock, as near as she could get to her birthplace, Clydebank, as her funnel which had been altered in one of her many refits would not allow her to pass under the Erskine Bridge. This was naturally one of the most closely followed steps on her way to retirement. She was accompanied by a Royal Naval destroyer *HMS Manchester* and some lucky enthusiasts went out on the heritage pleasure vessel *MV Balmoral* to visit her. There was even a fireworks display. Seeing her hull disappear down the Firth of Clyde for one last time, as I did, was a moving and unforgettable scene. The destination was round Scotland and down the east coast for Edinburgh and an anchorage in the shadow of that other icon, the Forth Rail Bridge, on 7 October. The next day she set sail for Newcastle, en route for Southampton, accompanied by a flotilla of small craft as an RAF fly-past thundered overhead.

So she said farewell to Britain but there was one final

Atlantic crossing in the company of her successor *QM2*. It did not end well. It might be fanciful to suggest the old lady was giving her fans one last demonstration of her headstrong personality but the fact is on 11 November she ran aground on a sandbank known as the Brambles Turn in Southampton water. Solent coastguards stated: "Five tugs were sent out to assist her getting off the sandbank, and she was pulled off just before 6.10 a.m. (*The grounding had occurred at 5.26 a.m.*) She had been refloated and was underway under her own power and heading back to her berth at Southampton. She had only partially gone aground and the tugs pulled her off." When safely tied up, farewell celebrations led by Prince Philip began and the champagne flowed and the canapes circulated while divers were in the murky waters of the port checking for damage. All was ok.

The next trip was a final voyage to Dubai where her new Arabian owners were based and where there were plans to turn her into a hotel ship. One of the saddest people to see this happen must have been Beatrice Muller, an 89-year-old who had been a permanent retirement resident on her for fourteen years. An uncertain future lay ahead but in Dubai it was a cause for celebration. Her arrival was marked by a fly-past by an Emirates A380 and the ruler of Dubai had his yacht out to greet her. Whatever grandiose plans there were for her, including one to get her back cruising, the global downturn blew them off course. She sat moored at the passenger terminal in Dubai for some months before work in a dry dock and a move to a berth at Port Rashid where she did not interfere with current cruise trade. The most attractive move of all, a return to the Clyde and refurbishment, seems in reality a mirage and the desert winds whistle over a sad and deteriorating icon just a few miles from one of the wealthiest places on the globe. Will no one help? Soon it will be too late. In her day she broke all sorts of records – in her day she was the largest, longest, tallest, widest and most expensive passenger liner ever built. She should not be allowed to rust to death.

14

A Secret Dash from Bombs on Clydebank to the Safety of the Big Apple

The building of the *QE2* was certainly a gamble for Cunard but it was not without precedent. Back in the thirties the company faced great problems – passenger numbers were falling, the economy was in depression, there had been an untidy merger with the White Star Line and another global conflict loomed on the horizon. Despite all this worrying background the board bravely commissioned two new super liners, the first two Queens, *Mary* and *Elizabeth*. The *Mary* was the largest man-made moveable object of her day. And amid all the awesome statistics, one remarkable little fact underlines why the accolade "Clydebuilt" was so powerful: each of the twin screws that powered her across the oceans was so accurately fitted that in dry dock they could be turned by hand. But it was not just in pure engineering skills that the workers in the Clyde yards excelled. They were also superb in the more artistic area of "fitting out". But as in any giant enterprise there was the occasional bad apple. Wryly I have to record that even in the thievery that happens in most workplaces one worker on the Queens must have operated on an Olympian scale – after arrest around thirty pilfered items were found in his possession. Among them, three book cases, six table settings, thirty yards of carpet, a toilet seat and two buckets!

The first *Queen Mary* was a masterpiece of Art Deco design (its main rival in the style stakes was the *Ile de France)*. Costs were not cut in the design department and it was said at the time that fifty-six different types of wood were used in cabins and public spaces. Carvers and artists used such as cedar and satinwood to create an ambiance of complete luxury. An excellent little Cunard book on the line's six Queens published in 2011 gives an insight into a life at sea long gone. It quotes a *Daily Telegraph* comment on the original *Queen Mary's* smoking room: "The keynote is solid comfort and snugness, characteristic of the best type of London or New York club, where deep leather armchairs in alcoves invite intimate conversations and a real coal fire blazes cheerfully in the grate." Not the sort of description that makes you long for the age of plastic and chrome! Around forty artists worked on the interiors and largely their work was praised though some, perhaps toffee nosed, critics thought that it was a tad too opulent for their taste and it reminded them of the flashy cinemas of the day, sweeping Busby Berkeley-style staircases and one too many chandeliers. However, it was a fit setting for famous passengers who included Edward VIII and Wallis Simpson, Bing Crosby, Fred Astaire, Audrey Hepburn, Elizabeth Taylor, Churchill and Dwight Eisenhower.

One of Cunard's most famous skippers, William Warwick, joined the line in 1937. Those lucky enough to get a seat at the Captain's Table on any of the great liners he commanded were guaranteed an entertaining time. He had a lot of tales to tell including one about one of his earliest voyages on a 400-feet-long vessel employed on what was called the pilgrim trade carrying Muslims to their holy places. It could take 1,800 passengers, almost as many as the original *Queen Mary*. But the culinary style on this old ship was far removed from that of fine dining on an ocean liner. Captain Warwick recalled that the pilgrims did their own cooking on concrete slabs on an upper deck and that one of his jobs was to ensure they did not light fires inside the ship. Captain Warwick, with his rugged looks and impressive beard, was like a character plucked from Hollywood's central casting to play the role of the skipper of a great liner. He looked the part. An eccentricity was that he liked to abbreviate his first name of William to Bil with one L.

When speechifying to land lubbers he often paid tribute to the engineering skills of Brown's. He used some unusual facts which resonated with his audiences. He would say: "It is not my practice to quote passengers carried or miles steamed to demonstrate the efficiency of these two liners. But rather to recall that for forty-four weeks out of every one of the last thirty years and for five days out of every seven of all those weeks, their propellers have revolved 160 times every minute driving a massive weight of 83,000 tons through the water at speeds of 30 to 35 miles per hour. To me they were the wonder of the age." Few would argue with that. Bil Warwick could smooth his way round a dinner table with the best of them night after night. But he always liked to remind passengers of Cunard's rules for masters laid down in 1847: "Keep yourselves always civil and kind to your passengers. Recollect they will value your services on deck, looking after their safety, more than talking with them in the saloons."

If the *Mary* was Art Deco the *Elizabeth* was, again according to Cunard, more Grand Elizabethan country house. In the current digital age the cry is "woodman save that tree". It was not heard when the *Elizabeth* was under construction. This time more than 100 tropical woods were used. Detailed thought went into even the construction of the bottom of the swimming pool: it was "lined with golden quartzite, a stone used in the days of the Pharaohs. Seen through seawater it gives the impression of a sandy pool"!

Earlier some of the wartime adventures of the *QE2* have been recounted. The original *Queen Elizabeth* also got into some scrapes of her own. On the outbreak of the Second World War, she lay unfinished in Clydebank, the hull complete, engines in place but not much else. The more than three thousand workers involved in her construction found the engines a convenient air raid shelter. This emphasised that she would be a juicy target for the Nazi bombers who were to almost bomb the town of Clydebank out of existence in deadly never to be forgotten air raids. The government thought the *Queen Elizabeth* should be moved to a place of safety as quickly as possible. The destination was New York, but that was a secret so closely guarded that even the skipper was well into an Atlantic dash to safety before he was allowed to open a sealed envelope containing the name of the final destination.

On 7 March 1940, she steamed upriver to the Big Apple and was berthed next to the *Queen Mary*, a sight to impress even the New Yorkers who were well used to seeing the great ships of the world berthed almost in the centre of their city. And not easily impressed. It took six months to get her truly shipshape, armed and fitted out as a trooper before she cast off for Singapore and her place in the war effort. She was a genuine workhorse of a troop ship, making more than sixty Atlantic crossings. At the end of hostilities she was converted back into a luxury liner running between Europe and the States. She continued in that role for almost twenty years before yet another refit and a new life as a fashionable cruise liner. The old beauty had a poignant, ignoble end in 1968. Of no further use on the oceans she was sold to Chinese owners to be converted into a floating university. During this work she caught fire and was burned out in Hong Kong harbour. The story of her sister the *Queen Mary* had similarities though the end was not so tragic or dramatic. She, too, was a successful troop carrier and helped in the Battle of the Atlantic before returning to commercial shipping service in 1947. She ended up as a museum ship in California in 1967.

15

Picnics on the West Coast and a Real Titan

The great Cunard liners are the ships perhaps most closely associated with Brown's. Yachts do not spring to mind when you mention the yard. (Though Clyde enthusiasts will tell you of great yacht builders in such places as Fairlie and Sandbank). But, of course Clydebank, if not famous for America's Cup winners, or losers like *Sceptre*, was the birthplace of *Britannia*, perhaps the most famous royal yacht of all. She was in the service of the Royal Family from 1954 to 1997. Apparently there was a tear or two in London when this elegant vessel was pensioned off and no replacement provided. No doubt the Royals were nostalgic in particular for the loss of their annual summer cruise round the Western Isles. This voyage often featured, when the mist rose off the Atlantic and the rain stopped, picnic trips ashore to a nearby beach by small boat. Gigha's beautiful west coast was a specially favoured spot.

Britannia was designed to be converted into a hospital ship in a war, but was never used in this role. It had a feature not common among ships of its size, around 6,000 tons – the tops of the masts folded over to allow passageway under canal bridges etc. The historian Peter Hennessy (also quoted in this book in his capacity as a submarine expert) is said to have talked of another possible war use: "It was the Queen's floating nuclear bunker . . . it would lurk in the sea lochs in north west Scotland; the mountains would shield it from Soviet radar and at night it would go quietly from one sea loch to another." That never happened.

The *Britannia* served her country well, steaming more than a million nautical miles in her career and some estimates claim that events held on board helped raise £3 billion for the treasury. But she was becoming elderly and expensive to maintain and an incoming Labour government decided the cost was simply too high. She went into retirement with her head held high – the final overseas mission was to bring the last governor of Hong Kong, Chris Patten, home after the handover of the colony to the People's Republic of China. The passenger list for this trip was less celebrity-studded than some earlier voyages. *Britannia* had played host in its day to four US presidents – Eisenhower, Ford, Reagan and Clinton. Diana and Charles also used it for a honeymoon cruise. Though it never went to war it did evacuate 1,000 refugees from a civil war in Aden. You wonder what these particular passengers made of the opulent surroundings.

In retirement she was listed in the National Historic Fleet. *Britannia's* fate was not without controversy. The natural place for her to end her days would have been on the Clyde not in Leith where she ended up, a place with less of a strong connection to shipbuilding than the Clyde. As ever, money talked and a berth was found for her in the Edinburgh port as part of a redevelopment of a run-down area. She has been a spectacular success as a tourist attraction with around 300,000 visitors a year. And her days as a celebrity magnet continue – Bond girl Ursula Andress held a birthday party on board. One claim to fame is that the yacht is the only place where you can take a peep through a glass window into a royal bedroom. I can confirm from personal experience that most visitors comment on how small it is, not much larger than a sleeper on a luxury train. The real opulence was kept for the large, hugely impressive dining room used to host foreign bigwigs on trips abroad to "sell" on behalf of British business. However, it could be observed that the stern cocktail bar was an item worthy of respect.

If not a seagoing item, the huge Titan crane which still stands in Clydebank at *Britannia*'s birthplace is a true Clyde icon. Like the royal yacht, it is a major tourist attraction, restored and opened to the public. The operator high in his cabin spent up to twelve hours a day at work, sustained only with his sandwiches and a flask of tea. He had a brilliant view of the great ships coming together beneath his feet. He also had a bucket up there with him for obvious purposes! Towards the end of the last century as Brown's went into decline the majestic Titan fell into disrepair and was a target for vandalism. But in its days of glory it helped build among others the mighty Cunarder Queens, *HMS Hood* and the *Britannia* itself. To become a museum of a slightly different kind was the welcome fate of Titan. As part of a rehabilitation enterprise in Clydebank it was restored to something akin to its full glory at a cost of almost £4 million and opened to the public in 2007. Ten years later it is attracting around 40,000 visitors a year.

Visitor satisfaction is high. A tour begins at a purser's office near the modern and un-shipyard-like Clydebank College building and is followed by a wee trip on a minibus to the foot of the Titan, now a listed historical structure. A lift then whisks you to the top for a wonderful vista of the Clyde and a close-up look at the workings of this engineering marvel. Its situation, just across the river from the end of the runway at Glasgow airport, also offers a splendid view of jets heading for touchdown or taking off. Landings from east to west almost let you have a look at the whites of the pilots' eyes. A reminder of the connection between shipbuilding and aviation is the fact that in the 1920s airships were built not so far from the modern runway at Inchinnan. Incidentally, before the military air base at Abbotsinch became the site of Glasgow International, the old airport, a few miles upriver at Renfrew, was a testing descent for pilots who had to pick a way through a forest of dockside cranes.

The Titan visited on a summer day is – jet noise apart – a place for calm reflection on the great days of the Clyde. But the waters that flow past the crane were a scene of tragedy in 2007 when three members of the crew of the tug *Flying Phantom* lost their lives when a tow upriver went wrong and their vessel overturned, trapped on a sandbank. And, of course, there is the appalling memory of the Clydebank blitz itself in the Second World War. On two nights in the spring of 1941, 528 Clydebankers lost their lives in attacks by German bombers. The massive Luftwaffe raids – more than 200 planes each night – practically wiped out the town with only a handful of properties not hit by the deluge of explosives. Amazingly, in raids intended to destroy shipbuilding on the upper Clyde, the Titan crane survived undamaged.

16

Ferries in "Boxes" and the Latest in Warships

The "build them up, break them down, rebuild thousands of miles away" technique did not just apply to the Irrawaddy ferries and Denny's featured in an earlier chapter. Still sailing, just, as I write is the remarkable *MV Ilala* which putters and stutters around Lake Malawi in East Africa providing a valuable link for passengers and cargo. The *Ilala* was built in Yarrow's in 1949 and shipped in parts to be assembled in Africa for the then Nyasaland Railways. It was quite a journey in itself. The bits and pieces boxed up back in Scotland were taken by cargo ship to Mozambique and then by road and rail to Chipoka. She began operating in 1951 and every week since, apart from maintenance periods, she has gone from her base at Monkey Bay in the south of the lake to Chilumba, almost in Tanzania, for turnaround back to the south, a distance of around 600 miles. Along the way she makes stops at important towns on the lakeside. It is a long life for a 600-ton diesel-powered vessel and an amazing tribute to her builders. Dodging the wrecker's yard for almost seventy years makes her something of a record breaker in shipping matters.

But you don't do that without showing your age, especially if you have survived several groundings, and damage to your steel hull requiring extensive repairs. And she has never been a ship that you would set your watch by. She does not always match the promises of her timetable and a delay of up to a day in her schedule is nothing unusual. She is a very valuable aid to transport in the area despite the eccentricity of arrivals and departures. Passengers and cargo get there eventually. The *Ilala* does not meet international requirements for passenger ships and she is to be replaced soon. If her successor gives anything like the service to her owners, Malawi Lake Services, that she has done it will be a major achievement.

A fascinating account of life on the *MV Ilala* is given by British historian, traveller and writer Oliver Ransford in his book *Livingstone's Lake*:

> Each day on board, amid the excited bell ringing, siren shrieks and hooting that seem inseparable from all maritime arrivals and departures, laughing crowds of Malawians line up on the *Ilala's* deck to disembark, cluttered up with baggage that includes bicycles, cages filled with squawking fowl, sewing machines and even tethered goats. They are ferried ashore in lighters to return an hour or so later crammed with another batch of passengers who quickly settle down in the cramped quarters to cards and singing and sleeping and the preparation of meals in little cooking pots. It all looks and sounds like a cross between Hampstead Heath on a Bank holiday and an Eastern market, but when the ship weighs anchor again the noise dies down and the first class passengers resume in their novels, their deck chairs and their worship of the sun.

All a bit different from life on a Clydebuilt Cunarder or British warship! Incidentally the name *Ilala* comes from a district in Zambia where it is said David Livingstone was first buried, underlining the Scottish connection.

The *Ilala* to be honest is now not a pretty sight. Nor a household name. She is not a large ship. But like some of the unglamorous products of the smaller Clyde yards she has made a mark particularly because of her longevity.

17

Tugs, Dredgers and the Pong of the Clyde

Nearer home the *Waverley* is an example of the fact that survival for long periods in a fast-changing world is one route to iconic status. It is not absolutely necessary to be a 200,000 toner or a Blue Riband holder. *Waverley* continues to be an asset to the burgeoning tourist industry in a Glasgow reinventing itself as a world-class destination for holidaymakers, particular what some might call "culture vultures". But it is an attractive thought that on the elegant old paddler the growing army of tourists can get away from the theatres, art galleries, museums and upscale restaurants for an hour or so of fresh air on the river, voyaging from Anderston Quay, in the centre of town, downriver to the Tail of the Bank and onwards towards the mouth of the firth to enjoy the spectacular scenery, and maybe even a tasty fish supper in the paddler's splendidly refurbished dining saloon – wine or beer optional. I am not certain, but I suspect a little dry white might be more to the taste of the new breed who sail "doon the watter". I have done this trip many a time with friends and visitors and one of the aspects they most mention is the number of scrapyards where the detritus of industrial southern Scotland lies piled high in several yards on both sides of the river awaiting ships to cart the ugly, but profitable, stuff away to recycling plants. The *Waverley* may sail into memorable scenery, but there is no disputing that the early miles from Anderston Quay are not too easy on the eye.

But the mountains of scrap metal and dozens of crumbling slipways and small weed-infested docks hide an interesting story. Many of the old smaller yards are now forgotten and the vessels they produced never came near the glamour of an Empress liner built in Fairfield's, a Cunarder at Brown's, or a super tanker at Lithgow's. But on reflection maybe the giants would never have reached the sea without the efforts of the minnows. A classic example is Simons and Lobnitz of Renfrew. Just west of the historic Renfrew ferry is one of the largest of the scrap heaps and it lies on the site of the old Lobnitz yard, close to where the Cart joins the Clyde. The Clyde has always had problems with silting, something that makes it less than ideal for building huge ships which often after launching have to be towed down-river for fitting out. A good example of the problem is that the old *Queen Mary* left Clydebank without its lifeboats in place in order to lessen the draft and make it possible to take it to a berth in Greenock for the final touches.

In the great days, dredgers, accompanied by barges into which they tipped grey muck, were a common sight to city-centre office workers having a lunchtime sandwich on one of the many upriver bridges. Old prams and furniture might sometimes have appeared in the dredge buckets, but despite the city's reputation for gangs and gangland, not too many bodies emerged from the brown water that flowed from the uplands of Lanarkshire to the sea. This seems to demolish the old "hard man" joke that the reason there are no glass bottom boats in Glasgow is that no one wants to see the bodies!

The Lobnitz family lived for a time in the quiet rural surroundings of Ayrshire, some distance inland from the frenetic energy and noise of the shipyards, in Chapeltoun House, near Stewarton, which became a hotel and restaurant much favoured by the moneyed of Ayrshire and Glasgow. The choice of a home in rich farmland was a tad unusual for a shipbuilding family since most of the great dynasties of the trade tended to build their stately piles nearer the river that made their fortunes.

Lobnitz as it was generally known on the Clyde was descended from Coulburn Lobnitz & Company, which was founded in 1874 at Renfrew. The Simons part of the Sunday name came from an amalgamation with an even older, adjacent, yard founded in 1860. Both companies specialised in the construction of dredgers and barges. And their combined expertise helped create improved dredging technology, some of which was exported worldwide. The fact that the Clyde was so prone to silting and the growing demand for deep water berths as shipbuilding in the area moved into its glory years meant there was a pretty constant demand on Lobnitz's front door. The yard finally closed in 1964 when the Far East and other markets began to buy elsewhere. But as well as the jaw-dropping total of 1,300 dredgers, many barges and tugs had emerged from the Renfrew site. The opening up of the Clyde owed much to the generally unsung work of the dredgers and hoppers. The hoppers, by the way, were often not dignified with a name; a humble number was good enough to identify these workboats.

Lobnitz was never a giant of the Clyde, other than by reputation, as battleships, liners and super tankers were not the right fit for the site, but the company did manufacture around sixty vessels for the Royal Navy from the First World War until 1945. These were mostly sloops, corvettes, minesweepers and boom defence vessels. One notable hull to emerge from the yard during this period was the first of a new class of purpose-built anti-submarine vessels called *HMS Saxifrage*. After the First World War, in 1921, she was renamed *HMS President* and began a new life moored on the Thames as a training ship for the Royal Naval Reserve; a sight of interest for any of the millions who visited London and were interested in ships.

Of a rather different sort of interest to Clydesiders was the *SS Shieldhall*, built in Renfrew in 1954, and for years her smartly painted grey hull, that seemed slightly incongruous considering her purpose, was familiar to river watchers. She was one of two boats, the other was the *Dalmarnock,* whose mission in life was to take treated sewage from the works near the site of the old Southern General Hospital many miles downriver to be dumped in deep water off Garroch Head. Vast quantities of what the polite would call waste was spewed into the waters and as it sank, slowly turning the sea into a memorable nasty brown colour, vast flights of seagulls swooped out of the sky for a free feast. The cargo was not the only thing that was free on the *Shieldhall*. The old Glasgow Corporation was responsible for the removal of the city's sewage, a major operation considering the population of around a million. It would be unthinkable now, but the solution was for years to spew the treated waste from holding tanks on the *Shieldhall* or *Dalmarnock* straight into the sea.

The Corporation, to its credit, tried to make the best of an unpleasant job by offering pensioner groups a free trip "doon the watter". As a young feature writer on the now long forgotten *Evening News* I was assigned to report on such a trip. Was the feature editor sending a message to his youngest writer? Hours on a sludge boat in the company of the elderly was not at first sight the task an ambitious young hack fancied. But I enjoyed it. Aft of the holding tanks for the sludge the *Shieldhall* had a small passenger area that was spotless – and relatively pong free – and here the "old yins" lucky enough to be offered the trip had a free cup of tea and some sandwiches and there was on occasion even dancing to an accordion. They had fun. It will come as no surprise to students of the Glasgow character that there were even tales of a wee half bottle or two being smuggled aboard in the voluminous pockets of the long woollen overcoats of the day. There was one snag – the pong of the cargo. I knew that the streets around the sewage works were regularly sprayed with chemically treated water vapour to ameliorate the smell for the benefit of the locals. But it was not entirely successful. However, on the river and in a wind when at top speed on the *Shieldhall*, I can honestly say that the unpleasant pong was swiftly left behind and there was instead a pleasant whiff of ozone.

The fame of the *Shieldhall* was such that it was often paid a tribute in the works of local folk musicians. One John Murphy had a couple of classic lines in his version: "A terrible aroma that had you in a coma" and "Pull your chain and we will answer your call". There was also humour on the river itself when skippers saw the familiar grey hull appearing. The crew of the sludge boats had to daily endure the signals from passing ships, with more acceptable and less odorous cargoes, enquiring with a straight face along the lines of, "Where are you bound? What is your cargo?" I don't remember noting it on my trip back in the sixties, but apparently the skipper's pea jacket was not the standard blue, but the sort of Corporation green affair more usually associated with Glasgow tram or bus drivers or the staff of the wee subway, the famous "Clockwork Orange" which runs in an underground circle in the city centre. The *Shieldhall*, like the *Waverley*, ended up on the UK's National Register of Historic Vessels. When the unhygienic insanity of dumping excrement by the ton into the open sea ended she was bought by a charity and operated pleasure cruises from Southampton. I don't know what they used the old sewage holding tanks for, but I am sure even in its new guise the passenger areas were not as spotless as they were in its old days of the "pong of the Clyde"!

The old Renfrew yard may be long gone but the name Lobnitz lives on. The history of the yards on the Clyde tends to be one of a long series of amalgamations, false starts and restarts, and when it closed in 1964, Lobnitz's goodwill and orders were bought by Alexander Stephens & Sons which four years later merged into Upper Clyde Shipbuilders which then collapsed in 1971. This allowed the formation of Lobnitz Marine Holdings operating as a marine engineering and naval architecture company.

Another builder specialising in dredgers was Fleming & Ferguson. This yard is perhaps now only of interest to those immersed in the minutiae of the history of shipbuilding, although it continued operating into the sixties after being founded as long ago as 1885. These days its main claim to fame is its location – Paisley – not a name that trips off the tongue when you are talking Clydebuilt. But there was more to this town than Paisley pattern shawls. The products of this shipbuilder in the Paisley yards were really "Cart built". The Black Cart and the White Cart, tributaries of the Clyde, meet at Inchinnan. Paisley is generally regarded as an inland location, but the White Cart flows through the town, more famous for linen and thread mills than shipbuilding. But at one time Paisley had around six yards, though naturally the size of the ships produced was severely limited by the narrowness of the river. This is a tad ironic considering

146

the fact that it was the usefulness of the proximity of the Cart's mouth, where it joins the Clyde, that helped Brown's on the north bank to launch giant warships and Cunarders near where the main river was itself only beginning to widen out. The giants were launched at a point where the stern could be dragged into the mouth of the extra width of the Cart. It is interesting, and now scarcely believable to anyone other than enthusiasts, to read of steamer services sailing from Paisley. Passenger service began in 1815 when the *Prince of Orange* (surely a berth nearer Rangers FC's Ibrox stadium would have been more suitable for a ship with such a name!) set off down the Cart the short distance to the Clyde and onwards to the open firth. Fifty or so years later a small fleet of steamers sailed from the textile town to the holiday resort of Rothesay on Bute on a daily basis. Small-scale navigation of the Cart continued, mostly coasters and puffers, until the seventies.

18

Glass Cases, Model Ships and Wee Jaunts Round the Harbour

The Clydebuilt legend has grown down the years aided largely by word of mouth from skippers, owners, seamen and passengers on the large and small ships that steamed out into the Atlantic. But the legend has also been burnished by a series of remarkable museum collections at home and abroad. Here in Scotland among the leaders in chronicling the Clyde's heritage for posterity are the Kelvingrove Art Gallery, the new Riverside Museum on the north bank of the river across from Govan, the Denny ship model experimental test tank at Dumbarton, the Scottish Maritime Museum at Irvine and a nice wee museum at the old Fairfield's site.

That legendary figure of Clyde shipbuilding Ross Belch was one of those behind the excellent Ayrshire museum which had a splendid refurbishment in 2016 and is particularly successful in attracting school children and interesting them in the history of shipbuilding in Irvine itself as well as paying tribute to the larger yards further up the firth on the

Clyde itself. Apart from the main exhibition centre a fine collection of old vessels, including the classic puffer *Spartan* and the steam yacht *Carola,* can be seen berthed on the riverside. A lot of thought and imagination has gone into this very unstuffy museum where the guides are a friendly lot who had often helped build or repair ships themselves. A flat in a nearby tenement, lived in during the 1920s, has been restored exactly the way it was. It is fascinating to watch a tour guide reach under the bed, extract a decorated china chamber pot and ask the astonished kids what it was used for! The reaction of the generation brought up on cell phones and computers at learning the role played in life by such an object in houses with only outdoor toilets was one of embarrassed disbelief.

Irvine's museum also recently hosted an exhibition of a selection of boats unlike those to be found anywhere else in the world – the paper boats of sculptor George Wyllie. George, also famous for a straw railway engine hanging from one of the Clyde's biggest cranes and then spectacularly set ablaze, and other eccentric items, not to mention his attractive paintings of puffers, indulged a wry sense of humour as befits a Clydesider; he was born in Glasgow but later lived in Gourock. Of an 80-feet paper boat he created he wrote: "It appears the delicate craft was built in Glasgow on the River Clyde for the Origami Line whose president said that it had saved his company from folding up." That sense of humour also surfaced in another of his works entitled "Slap and Tickle Machine". George was not just a local artist, he was well known worldwide – his famous giant paper boat even sailed up the Hudson River in New York to berth outside the World Trade Centre.

Fascinating as the Scottish Maritime Museum is in my view there is still room for a major museum nearer Glasgow on the river itself. As mentioned previously, the brilliance of the exterior design of the relatively new Riverside Museum is not matched by the interior. It mixes some interesting maritime memorabilia with static displays of locomotives, cars and carts. There is much good social history in this museum, but it has a scatter-gun approach. The main maritime attraction is, of course, Glasgow's Tall Ship, the *Glenlee* now remarkably well restored and docked just outside the main exhibition area. There is also a nice little collection of small Clyde ships and ferries just outside the walls of the museum where the Kelvin joins the Clyde around the site of the old A. & J. Inglis yard. But you could hardly describe it as a blockbuster exhibition. The story of the Clyde deserves more than one iconic vessel from the great days moored near its birthplace. What is really needed is the chance to take trips up and down the river other than a fast blast on a RIB or a nostalgic trip on the *Waverley*. There seems to me a great opportunity for an entrepreneur to run river trips in the style of those on offer on the Thames or the Seine. And certainly there is a need for a larger scale museum specialising in shipbuilding history.

In peregrinations around far-flung parts as a journalist I have been lucky to visit some of the world's great maritime museums in places like San Francisco, Hawaii, Hong Kong and Auckland. All celebrate to some extent the Clydebuilt legend. The best to my mind is Auckland. New Zealand likes to be described as the land of the long white cloud. And on a sunny summer day the white clouds of the sails of the yachts that throng the bay are as impressive as those drifting overhead.

As I write, five examples of the great days of Clydebuilt sail are still afloat in museums around the world – the *Glenlee* in Glasgow, of course, the *Falls of Clyde* in Hawaii, the *Balclutha* in San Francisco, the *Moshulu* in Pennsylvania and *Pommern* in Mariehamn, Finland. Today these beautiful examples of shipbuilding are usually referred to as "museum ships" though in fact the *Moshulu* is now a floating restaurant. The term "windjammer", used to categorise such ships, is to my mind the most attractive. But almost all tall ships are often loosely called "clippers" even if they were never as beautiful or as fast as true American clippers or the British vessels that took part in the China tea races. The name clipper seems to have evolved from the need to "clip" along at speed with certain cargoes such as tea from China that needed to get to a particular market. Fast.

There is a lot for the sail enthusiast to see in Auckland – examples of the great ocean racing yachts, though sadly not a full rigged ship. In fact one of the most interesting exhibits in the New Zealand Maritime Museum has no sails at all. But it has a Scottish connection. It is something of a rarity in the modern maritime world, an unusual floating steam crane called the *Rapaki*. The explanatory notes on both floating exhibits and those inside the museum displayed in Auckland are the best of their type I have found. The Clyde's worldwide reputation is alluded to in the information on the *Rapaki*. Visitors are informed that the builders were a "Paisley, Scotland firm and that the Fleming & Ferguson yard and engine works had gained a worldwide reputation for quality small ships and steam reciprocating machinery". This is the firm mentioned earlier as specialist builders of dredgers as was their near neighbour Simons and Lobnitz. The Auckland museum also points out that the unusual vessel was equipped with a crane constructed by Sir William Arrol & Co., the builders of the Forth Bridge and the famous giant Titan crane so prominent on Clydeside. The *Rapaki* was an 80-ton self-propelled crane ordered by Lyttelton Harbour Board in 1925. The cost was £42,000 and the vessel was to meet the port's demands for a heavy lift crane. It was built in record time and on 26 April 1925, she set sail for the new world under the command of a delivery master, Captain H. Liddell Mack. The museum records: "She made her delivery voyage to New Zealand under her own steam. The voyage, which took 109 days via the Panama Canal, was an eventful one, and *Rapaki* faced a number of storms and shortages of food and coal. She was believed lost for a time when she almost ran out of coal on the East Coast of the North Island, eventually limping into Gisborne. Finally *Rapaki* arrived in Lyttelton on 27 July, during a strong southerly gale and high seas. After a period of maintenance, on 14 October 1926, she was ready to work."

Rapaki spent most of her working life at Lyttelton but saw war service in Auckland, and in the Pacific. She was retired from service in 1988 and purchased by the New Zealand Maritime Museum in 1993. Towed to Auckland by a navy tug she has since performed the dual role of floating break-water and static display.

Rapaki has a unique welded "Scotch Boiler" but the logistics of firing her systems by coal are immense, expensive and difficult in the sunshine of a brightly coloured city-centre location. Clouds of black smoke produced when the 145 tons of coal in her bunkers are burned are not particularly welcome in Auckland's tidy and clean harbour! She was steamed under coal for the last time in February 2001. The museum notes: "The 'Live Steam Project' commenced with work to make the machinery spaces readily accessible to the public. The propeller shafts have recently (July 2003) been disconnected and modifications to the pipe-work have commenced to enable the main engines and auxiliary machinery to be operated (under no load) using steam from a self-contained boiler powered by gas or diesel."

This is an exemplary example of restoration of industrial

heritage, but no one, not even the veterans who worked on the project or the most enthusiastic of steam power enthusiasts or her builders back on Clydeside, could claim that she is a thing of beauty. No matter, the many galleries of this museum are stuffed with sailboats of extreme beauty, which hardly comes as a surprise since it is said that at one time or another New Zealand has held every significant sailing trophy in the world. There is also an impressive collection of maritime art. It is worth a full day of anyone's time. And if after an hour or so you feel like fresh air you can get out on the water yourself and get right in there among the hundreds of yachts by touring the harbour in the museum's restored scow *Ted Ashby*.

I love maritime museums and have indulged myself by visiting some of the best in the world. But there is one ship that tells so much of what Clydebuilt meant in the great days of sail that you will not find in any museum: the *Grace Harwar*. Built by William Hamilton & Co. in Port Glasgow in 1889 for a London owner (though it spent much of its forty-six years in Scandinavian hands) it is the flawed heroine of one of the best books on the sea ever written, *By Way of Cape Horn* by Alan Villiers. Villiers says: "She is a steel full rigged ship of 1,749 tons neither big for a full rigged ship nor small. She was average." He noted that she was neither a clipper nor even a fast ship, but neither was she a stodgy drifter. She had good lines and could transport 3,000 tons of cargo across the wildest of the planet's oceans. Her three tall masts had a "graceful loftiness" and her bow was "lovely". The young adventurer said she was a "true sister of the Horn". She used no power of any kind other than the wind apart from a small petrol winch to help load and unload through the main hatch.

The still photographs of her in her heyday are impressive. And shots of the crew high aloft changing sail as the vessel ploughed along and rolled in huge swells can almost give you an attack of vertigo just looking at them on the printed page.

In 1929 Villiers, a newspaper man and sail enthusiast then working in Tasmania, had signed on for one of the last great voyages round the Horn under sail. It is a remarkable adventure story that captured in words, and some rough-and-ready film footage, what life in such a ship was like. Before he was paid off at the end of the voyage in Glasgow, many months later at the end of that year's grain race from Australia, he had developed affection for the old vessel despite the tragic loss of his Australian friend on board and other desperate moments at sea. On this voyage she sailed with a crew of thirteen hands before the mast to set and stow the gigantic sails in all weathers. And this was one more than was needed thought the owner. Six of the crew could be classed as able seamen and the others "boys" with an average age of nineteen. Three had never been to sea before. Villiers notes that the significance of the figure thirteen was not remarked on though if any of the crew who set off around the Horn had done some research they might not have been so keen to set sail. The *Grace Harwar* for all her good points had a reputation as a man-killer. In 1907, under the command of Captain C. S. Hudson, the ship was sailing from Australia to Tocopilla, Chile. Captain Hudson's young wife was on board. Already suffering from tuberculosis, she died off the coast of Chile. The ship returned empty to Australia with Mrs Hudson's body in the ballast. Supposedly, Mrs Hudson put a curse on the ship before dying – that it would kill one man on every voyage. And indeed one of the crew, a friend and colleague of Villiers, died on the 1929 voyage in an accident.

As mentioned, Alan Villiers was paid off in Glasgow at the end of the *Grace Harwar*'s epic voyage with happy memories of good times as well as bad. But any rose-coloured dreams the young Aussie had when thinking of a life at sea were destroyed by the reality. Life under sail on the *Grace* may not have been as bad as some crewmen experienced during the last days of sail. But it was no picnic. Indeed, talking generally of life on one of the last of the great sailing ships, Villiers wrote: "Apprentices in particular were worse off than dogs since if they had been dogs they would at least have been able to crawl off somewhere for a night's rest, now and again." The apprentices, some as young as fifteen, did all the dirty work. They attended to sails high on the masts, sometimes sent aloft on their own. At times the tasks assigned to them by drunken skippers and incompetent officers verged on murder and many did die – thrown into the sea or falling to a painful death on the deck while trying to manhandle sails sometimes 170 feet high above huge seas. They were the ones who cleaned out the lavatories and pigsties (a term for a kind of room on a ship, harking back to the early days of sea travel where ships carried live pigs as a source of fresh meat). They polished brass and hauled coal for the cook's fires. They were not allowed to splice ropes or even to steer. Food was short and voyages long.

Villiers is perhaps the best-known chronicler of the last days of sail, but he was not the only one to preserve in detail the way of life of those hard days. Another old seadog, Captain Vincent Large, put pen to paper, to capture for posterity his adventures as a windjammer apprentice. As a boy he had a robust appetite. Just as well, for the food served on his vessel, the *Shakespeare*, was a million nautical miles away from the healthy and tasty menus of today's liners or even freighters. Vincent Large remarks that sailing ship men had an old saying that God provided the food and the devil the cook. On the *Shakespeare* he was of the opinion that the devil provided both the food and the cook.

He detailed his three favourite dishes: "Cracker Hash", "Dandyfunk" and "Dog's body". If this is the top end of the fare served you wonder what the everyday stuff was like. There were many variations on the recipes for these odd dishes but the young Large gives the reader his version of how to make them. He considered himself a dab hand at both "Cracker Hash" and "Dandyfunk". The main ingredient for both was powdered ship's biscuits instead of flour. First the more obvious large and juicy weevils were handpicked from the biscuits, which were then placed in a canvas bag and smashed to a crumble using a belaying pin as a hammer. For the "Cracker Hash" some dripping need to be wheedled out of the cook and scraps from the infrequent servings of pork saved. Pepper if obtainable was considered an exotic spicing that much improved the dish.

Large writes that the biscuit powder was mixed up with the chopped pork to create a sort of dough which was patted down on a tin plate and any available bacon fat placed on top ready for the oven. Unlike this unsavoury-sounding savoury, "Dandyfunk" was a kind of cake, again using powdered ship's biscuits this time mixed with brown sugar, marmalade and butter. Great with tea on the rare calm Sunday afternoon, remarks Large. What was "Dog's Body" was left to the reader's imagination. Incidentally, his book, *Windjammer 'Prentice*, went to some length to describe the dangers of scurvy and the value of lime juice. An 1865 law made the consumption of this compulsory on long voyages. According to Vincent Large: "When a man developed scurvy his mouth and gums swelled, his teeth fell out and all parts of his body became infected. In serious cases death was almost inevitable." The juice of raw potatoes was also considered effective, but lime juice was more convenient. It was so important that if a sailor refused to take his ration it had to be noted in the log.

All serious stuff. But the old salt Large dripped some humour into the recipe for a good memoir. He told of a voyage from Melbourne to the Horn. Many crew members would jump ship in Australia attracted by the weather and the opportunities in a new and expanding country, not to mention the thought that almost anything was better than a trip rounding the Horn battling for weeks on end the incessant gales of sleet and freezing rain. Such a desertion left his ship needing a new mate. One was recruited from an unattractive list of applicants. It was an easy sail down to the Tasman Sea, but then they hit dirty weather. One evening the new mate came on watch in heavy wind and rain. Just before reaching the open deck he stopped and fiddled with something he carried, watched by curious shipmates. When he reached the fore part of the poop the second mate turned to hand over the watch to the new man and stared in utter astonishment: the mate stood calmly in front of him holding an umbrella to shelter from the wind and lashing rain. It was a sight probably never seen before or after on a windjammer. But it did not impress the skipper. At the first opportunity, in the next port, the new mate was put ashore to be replaced by a more robust character. The captain and crew were English but any Clydesider, never mind Glaswegian hard man, would understand that the open deck of a sailing ship was no place for such a "sissy" as his mates had branded the Umbrella Man!

Perhaps not surprisingly, considering the reputation of Clydebuilt ships, the Scots who went to sea rose above the stereotype of the villainous ship master. Villiers remembered a spell on a ship bound for Tasmania largely crewed by Scots who spent time in port drinking whisky and "blowing wailing tunes on a thing they called a chantey (chanter I presume!) or something." He preferred them drinking whisky.

The old *Grace Harwar* was the slowest of the full-rigged ships in the 1929 grain race taking 136 days from Wallaroo to Queenstown where she lay for a bit before a tow to the Clyde. She had been blown off course by around 1,000 miles, slowed by leaks and years of marine growth on the rusting hull, and generally her old age. For the last leg of the journey she was pulled by a sturdy tug called *Strongbow*. The last days of her eventful voyage were a contrast to what had gone before. The weather was fine, the wind gentle, and the crew even found the strength to raise a sail on occasion to make life easier for the tug. On Saturday, 14 September 1929 they entered the Firth of Clyde. Alan Villiers painted a vivid word picture of the firth so different from how it is today: "It was a glorious day and we enjoyed it to the full. Many big steamers passed us by, Cunarders, White Stars, and Anchor liners bound to America, the Far East, Australia and Peru. They all came close and cheered the old full-rigger as we passed up the Clyde behind our tug. At the Tail of the Bank another tug came to help us, and with one tug astern and the other ahead, and the decks given over to the charge of a cheerful pilot we carried on into the night right up the river to our berth. Shortly after midnight the tugs with a great deal of congested manoeuvring and shrieking of their whistles nosed us into a remote corner of the Prince's dock, right beneath the towering sides of a big Furness Withy steamer." For Alan Villiers one adventure was finally over. And the *Grace Harwar* only memory.

One of the most famous of the full-rigged ships built on the Clyde to make it to a gentle retirement as a museum, rather than succumb to the ignominy of death by ship-breaker or rock and storm, was the *Balclutha* which lies in a spectacular setting in San Francisco. More than Tony Bennett have left their heart in this beautiful place and taken home memories of crab rolls on Fisherman's Wharf or the fabled Ghirardelli chocolate manufactured in the city in a factory claiming to be the only place in the States where the product is made in one place, "from bean to bar". Or maybe they have even enjoyed a boat trip out in the bay to Alcatraz and a visit to the one-time home of Al Capone. Frisco has a lot going for it tourist-wise, but to any Scots passing through, a visit to the waterfront and the *Balclutha* is a must. This vessel, with a distinctive grey hull similar to Glasgow's Tall Ship, was built as a general trader by Charles Connell & Company in Scotstoun in 1886 for Robert McMillan of Dumbarton. It filled the bill superbly and hauled cargoes as varied as timber, rice, wool, grain and wine across the oceans. She rounded Cape Horn seventeen times in thirteen years and also took part in the Chilean nitrate trade, dirty work for sailors and ships, which was the fate of so many windjammers in the dying days of sail. The name *Balclutha* is the subject of various interpretations. The Clutha connection with Glasgow is obvious and some maritime historians say the name means "City on the Clyde" derived from the Gaelic *Baile Chluaidh*. Others say it came from the town of the same name in New Zealand.

Perhaps some of her most productive years were spent operating out of Frisco under a new name, *Star of Alaska*. In this role she sailed north to Alaska in the spring carrying supplies for the fishermen and cannery workers returning south in the autumn with tinned salmon. It is interesting that for most of their lives the last of the windjammers were inadequately crewed as owners tried to save expense as steam was beginning to drive them off the seas. But in the salmon trade *Balcultha/Star of Alaska* had around 200 crew and passengers rather than a mere twenty or so crew of her early days. In the 1930s the end was in sight. A new owner renamed her again as the *Pacific Queen* and there was a brief flurry of new glory when she was used in the film *Mutiny on the Bounty* with Clark Gable and Charles Laughton. But it was downhill thereafter as age and a hard life took their toll. For a while she was an exhibition ship and even hosted tourists visiting a "pirate ship". A touch tacky. However, now the fully restored vessel sits splendidly alongside Hyde Street Pier at the San Francisco Maritime National Historical Park and enjoys the status given to her by the Americans as National Historic Landmark. But every now and again the dignity of such a title gets a little dose of Saturday night fun in the form of a Sea Shanty Singalong. Rum anyone?

A particularly beautiful example of the full-rigged ship, one that almost ended her days in San Francisco alongside the *Balclutha*, is the *Falls of Clyde*. I boarded her in Honolulu some years ago and even motionless and moored to a dock in the harbour she was a beautiful sight. But to appreciate her special attraction she was best seen at sea. A small booklet *Famous Ships of the Clyde* published in 1993 quoted a lyrical description of what she looked like in her heyday. A young German sailor, Fred Klebingat, wrote of seeing her gleaming white sails filled with a strong breeze and glinting in a morning sun: "We assembled aft, the captain and his mates, the watch on deck and the watch below, even the cook, just to admire her as she crossed our course astern. Her sleek brown hull was ornamented at the bow with a graceful figurehead, a lady in white, who with unseeing eyes gazed out over the path ahead." Young Fred was at the beginning of his career but the *Falls of Clyde* was to feature in his future career when he served as mate on the ship he so admired.

Scotland has a reputation of a place where rain is never in short supply. And the black clouds that so often scud overhead ensure that you are never far from a waterfall. Which was handy for the Falls shipping line. *Falls of Clyde* (the actual falls near New Lanark are well worth a visit, especially in the winter snow and ice) is the only survivor of a fleet that had nine vessels all named after Scottish waterfalls. She was built at Russell's in Port Glasgow and designed by a young man with a name that has resonated down the years in the history of shipbuilding – William Todd Lithgow. This talented young scion of the great family became the sole partner of Russell's which eventually became known as Lithgow's.

There is a touch of irony in the fact that this good-looking windjammer was destined to make a different sort of nautical history by becoming one of the first of that often unloved vessel, the bulk oil carrier. But that was in the future. After she slipped into the river in 1879 her maiden voyage took her to Karachi and in the next twenty years or so she sailed the world – without the aid of oil! – to the likes of Calcutta, Rangoon, Bombay, Auckland, Melbourne and San Francisco and points in between. Everywhere she went she had admiring glances from the enthusiasts round the world who, sometimes in the most unlikely of places, followed the fate of the tall ships.

Her own fate held some unhappy adventures in store. After around seventy trading voyages worldwide she was sold to the famous American Matson line which was for years the main link for passengers and cargo to the Hawaiian islands. The *Falls of Clyde* was to end her days in Honolulu, but that was years off. Her early years with Matson were spent taking passengers bound for the surf and grand hotels of Waikiki beach and the other islands and the delights of the famous sunsets. The holds were filled with less glamorous general cargo including live-stock. This was in the days before America took control of the islands and she flew the Hawaiian flag proudly. This lasted for around eight years and then, in 1907, she was converted into a bulk oil carrier. Until then oil had mostly been carried in five-gallon cans.

Carrying oil kept her busy during the First World War and later in 1922 she had a further conversion to become a floating oil depot in Alaska. The next move was to be the ignominy of being sunk as part of breakwater in Vancouver harbour. But up popped that lyrical sailor Fred Klebingat, by now a captain, who thought the planned fate of a ship still in relatively good order a mistake. How right he was. Captain Fred had the idea that the maritime museum in San Francisco might make a good final berth. It was not to be, but eventually Honolulu became interested and a classic campaign to save an item of historic interest was begun. Local press and radio did their bit, children rattled cans, and money was raised for restoration by the local Bishop Museum. Sir William Lithgow, grandson of her designer, helped with the restoration. And for a number of years she was a tourist attraction in Honolulu harbour much admired by all who saw her. But her story still had a few turns ahead, not all of the "lived happily ever after" type. When I visited her, her paintwork was bright, the varnished rails and polished brass work shone under the almost constant Hawaiian sun. Now she is a sad sight. The original restoration ran out of steam and today rust splatters her steel hull and even viewed from afar the decay is obvious. Close up the toll taken by the years is deeply depressingly. It is truly sad that an iconic vessel which has been on the United States National Register of Historic Places since 1973 (she was declared a US National Historic Landmark in 1989) is in such a condition especially in a country that in many other areas lavishes millions of dollars on conservation projects.

The deterioration is, it seems, a result of not spending relatively small sums on preventative maintenance after the initial restoration. She has not been in dry dock for years and there are claims that sand blasting to clean up the hull in fact damaged her. There has been what folk in her Greenock birthplace would call a stushie about how the money originally raised to preserve her was spent. The Bishop Museum, her long-time owners, seemed unable to handle the project any more in 2008 and they said they had plans to sink her by the end of the year unless private funds were raised for her perpetual care. So that year ownership was transferred to a non-profit group called Friends of the Falls of Clyde who intended to restore her. But that happy ending seems a distant prospect. In late 2016, it was reported that the Hawaii Department of Transportation has revoked her permit to moor at Pier 7 on the grounds of "safety and security risks to port users".

The *Falls of Clyde* is 138 years old and its place in maritime history is more secure than the future of the ship itself. It is the only surviving iron-hulled four-masted sailing ship in the world, itself a reason for saving her. She also has another claim to fame as the only surviving sail-driven oil tanker in the world, a description that does not capture the beauty of her design. A million and a half dollars needs to be raised to dry dock her as a first stage of full restoration. Fund-raising goes on. Surely America has enough wealthy folk with super yachts, costing into the hundreds of millions, to find the cash. Some of the US's yachting billionaires even own two luxurious seagoing gin palaces. One even uses his second super yacht to follow in the wake of his favourite, principally to carry the luggage of his guests so that the Louis Vuitton suitcases don't get in the way of his guests' fun. With folk like that around America should not allow the shame of scuttling the *Falls of Clyde* to happen. The owners of the glitzy yachts claim to love the sea. Let them open their chequebooks to prove it.

There is a Clydebuilt full-rigged sailing ship that is remarkable both in its story itself and the fact that it is largely forgotten despite being a real speedster worthy of a greater place in maritime history than it seems to have. In his book *Boy Aloft* Gavin Craig, who sailed on her, tells of the hard life of the apprentices as mentioned earlier. He is more succinct than most however and I like his definition of the life: "Wind, wetness and brutality". His ship was the *Lancing* constructed by the Govan yard of Robert Napier in 1866. Like the *Falls of Clyde*, which was converted to an oil tanker, the *Lancing* was vastly altered during her life at sea, in her case from a steam ship to a sailing ship! Surely a unique happening.

She was originally a transatlantic mail steamer operated by a French firm called Compagnie Générale Transatlantique of Paris and named *Pereire*. She served for some years as a speedy and successful vessel on the often turbulent Atlantic waters. But she was to have no long and quiet life. Instead, an eventful career lay ahead. In 1881 she was in use as a troop transporter and caught fire and was scuttled in Tunis harbour. The French Navy tried to torpedo her but the two-inch thick Clyde steel defied them and she had to be scuttled to put out the fire. However, she was raised and refitted and put back into service, but six years later she was stranded off St Naziare and so badly damaged that she was sold to a London firm who, no doubt impressed by her graceful and speedy hull, ripped out the steam engines and converted her to a four-masted full-rigged sailing ship now named *Lancing*! This was seriously swimming against the tide as around the world steam was driving sail into history.

She then had a string of owners, including Norwegians who still hung on to sail for years after the rest of the world had converted to steam, before being scrapped in Genoa in 1925. But in her days of sail this remarkable vessel managed to do something no other sailing ship had done. According to maritime historian Basil Lubbock the *Lancing* managed an average of 18 knots over seventy-two hours on a voyage from New York to Melbourne, something Lubbock claims no other commercial sail-powered vessel has ever managed.

Lancing in fact created a wheen of records under sail including a voyage from Nova Scotia to Greenock in fifteen days in 1916. At times she was clearly the fastest sailing ship in the world. It seems a little sad to me that when folk with an interest in the sea gather in harbour-side pubs around Clydeside the talk is more of the glamorous Cunard Queens with their stylish lounges and luxury accommodation than this great workhorse of a ship, built just upriver from the birthplace of the great battleships and liners. The *Lancing* deserves to be better remembered.

On the subject of maritime museums I must say that as someone who relocated from the southside Glasgow suburbs to Kintyre I regret that I have never, so far, visited the celebrated San Diego museum. One of the star attractions there is an elegant steam yacht, *Medea*, which was built by Stephens of Linthouse, that in past years sailed the waters of the Kilbrannan Sound, just outside my Carradale home, taking members of the Macalister Hall family to their rather more impressive domicile, Torrisdale Castle, in the early years of the last century. Like many another old pile in Scotland, the castle should be more accurately described as an historic mansion house, though its owner

General Keith Macalister Hall had an impressive military pedigree.

San Diego is proud of its Scottish exhibit and in promotional material it is lavished with praise:

> Named after a Greek mythological figure, the *Medea* has a past almost as colourful as her namesake. Originally, the steam yacht was built in 1904 for William Macalister Hall of Torrisdale Castle, Scotland. Built of steel and furnished with imported teak and quarter-sawn oak, the *Medea* is an impressive and beautiful little boat. Macalister Hall, a wealthy landowner and British Army officer, used *Medea* mainly for social occasions and hunting trips around the isles and lochs of western Scotland. By the beginning of the First World War, she was in the hands of the man who built her, John Stephen. Later during the war, she was purchased by the French Navy and converted to a gunboat named *Corneille*. Armed with a 75mm gun, depth charges and an observation balloon, she operated as a convoy escort for French sailing ships. After the war she resumed her old name and returned to British colours. Owned by members of the Parliament, she often cruised the Mediterranean Sea.

Early in the Second World War, *Medea* joined the Royal Navy as a barrage balloon vessel at the mouth of the River Thames. Later she went back to Scotland and was used by the Norwegian Navy, based there as an accommodation ship for Norwegian commando officers.

By 1946 *Medea* was back in British civilian service, cruising off Cornwall and the Isle of Wight. During the 1950s and 1960s, she had four different owners, including Job Longson Wild, her owner prior to the Second World War. In those post-war years she served at her owners' pleasures. From 1966 to 1969 she was in charter service, until her Swedish owners took over in 1969. By that time,

Medea was a tired old boat, but she was still pretty enough to capture the attention of oilman Paul Whittier, who had steamed aboard similar vessels in his youth. In 1971, Whittier purchased, restored and donated *Medea* to the Maritime Museum of San Diego. This amazing gift arrived in San Diego on 14 July 1973.

Today *Medea* still cruises the Bay on special excursion cruises for invited guests. Although she is not permitted to carry paying passengers, she is open dockside to welcome all visitors to the Maritime Museum.

The Torrisdale Castle and estate on the east coast of Kintyre is currently being revitalised under the new generation of Macalister Halls and visitors can get entertaining information on the *Medea* and the intriguing history of the family. As well as this there is the chance to visit a renowned tannery and, in a recent innovation, the opportunity to buy a craft gin called Beinn a Tuirc (Hill of the Wild Boar) brewed on the premises.

19

No "Bevvying", Great Speeches and the Fight for a Dream

This idiosycratic, somewhat personal, look at the story of shipbuilding on the Clyde has mostly examined the yards individually. The enterprises founded by the legendary families like the Lithgows, Dennys, Yarrow's, Scotts, A. and J. Inglis, Browns, Stephen's and others spent years competing for orders from the British merchant shipping industry and the Royal Navy in the great days of the Clyde. And the world tended to come to them for everything from river ferries to dredgers, tugs, tankers and the finest of ocean liners. On the commercial front it was a case of every yard for itself, chasing orders and building reputations. But in the later years of the last century, after two world wars and a recession, changes in world shipbuilding hit the Clyde hard. Competition from yards in the Far East and eastern Europe combined with ageing facilities and heavily unionised workforces, sometimes almost completely out of the control of the "bowler hats" in the management and boardrooms, made it clear there had to be changes. In the good old days, a veteran draftsman remarked to me that if you opened a window in the design department an order flew in.

It was not like that in the sixties, seventies and eighties. No longer did the world come to the Clyde. The salesmen from the yards had to roll up their sleeves, jump on a new-fangled Boeing jet and scour the world for orders. Often it was not fair competition as Japanese and other yards took full advantage of cheap labour, and sometimes massive government subsidies, to gain the work. The Clyde's sadly growing reputation for ugly and divisive industrial relations did not help. The union problem was so severe that a welder told a newsman that the "governor", Sir Robert Easton, who managed to steer Yarrow's successfully through the turbulent waters of the time, was due credit for transforming a one-time "holiday camp" back into a vibrant enterprise.

In the late 1960s it was clear to everyone in the industry, the general public and even national politicians that there was a need for drastic action. As is the way of governments, various reports were commissioned to provide an analysis of the problem and suggest solutions. The Geddes Report of 1966 and the subsequent Shipbuilding Industry Act 1967, which was sponsored by the Ministry of Technology under Tony Benn, pointed to the obvious: consolidation and cooperation. Benn's department in particular suggested dividing the UK industry into regional groups to use integration of resources to achieve economies of scale and improve the search for orders. There were to be grants from the Shipbuilding Industry Board. In Scotland this led to the creation of Upper Clyde Shipbuilders (UCS) in 1968. Five major yards were involved in the consortium: Fairfield (Govan Division), Alexander Stephen's (Linthouse Division), Connell (Scotstoun Division) and John Brown & Company (Clydebank Division). Yarrow's was an "associate subsidiary". The government had a minority stake of 48.4 per cent and provided interest-free loans over the first three years. The order book for the consortium stood at nearly £90 million at the time. In its relatively short history UCS had many ups and downs and to this day there is deep argument as to whether or not it was a "success".

In one way it was an outstanding success – it transformed industrial relations. And saved some yards and jobs. And that was down to a group of men as outstanding in their own field as were the many legends on the management side. Before the consortium was created in 1968 only insiders were aware of the names of such union activists in the yards as Jimmy Airlie, Jimmy Reid, Sammy Barr and Sammy Gilmore. Soon their names and their concept of a "work-in" rather than constant strikes were generating headlines nationwide. The members of this remarkable group were at the time all relatively young and all members of the Communist Party of Great Britain. One attribute of those who waved the Red Flag worldwide was the ability to make speeches that motivated millions of workers in the fight against capitalism. On the Clyde and beyond, Airlie and Reid were noted public speakers able to hold thousands in their thrall as they fought to save jobs and lives. Reid was, of course, the ultimate master of the mass meeting. With Airlie, perhaps the more strategic thinker of the two, they made impressive leaders.

Jimmy Reid in particular was superb. In later years, now part of the media himself rather than in its spotlight, he was a colleague of mine at Glasgow's *Herald*. He was wonderful company, full of humanity and humour, constantly spilling out perceptive thoughts. Always concerned about people. Perhaps that was his success as a public speaker – what you saw was what you got, whether the audience was hundreds of workers in their oil-stained overalls and bunnets or just a handful of hacks in a bar. The tactics of the shop stewards around Reid and Airlie worked well with the public who rallied to their cause in thousands. The public sympathy for the work-in was massive. Demonstrators took to the streets in thousands to back the workers. Indeed one rally was said to have been attended by 80,000 people. Tony Benn flew north to address them and former shipyard workers like Matt McGinn entertained in between the speeches of the firebrands. The public also showed where their hearts lay by dipping into their pockets to help sustain the workers. And celebrities around the world sent cheques. At one committee meeting of the organisers, Jimmy Reid was able to tell the guys round the table that there was a contribution of £5,000 from John Lennon, which prompted the comment from a presumably elderly worker and no fan of the Beatles: "But Lenin's deid".

Jimmy Reid's oratory came to public notice right from the start of the dispute. He wanted to show the continuing viability of the yards by completing what orders the yards had until the Tory government went back on its plan to cut all state subsidy with the loss of around 6,000 jobs. Reid declaimed, in a speech that was to become famous: "We are not going to strike. We are not even having a sit-in strike. Nobody and nothing will come in and nothing will go out without our permission. And there will be no hooliganism, there will be no vandalism, and there will be no bevvying (drinking) because the world is watching us, and it is our responsibility to conduct ourselves with responsibility, and with dignity and maturity." He was playing for high stakes and on subsidies he initially won. Edward Heath backed down and for the next three years the government chipped in support of almost £100 million.

That famous speech was an elegant plea to save the jobs and way of lives of those Jimmy Reid had grown up with

171

and worked with. But his oratory could move into a wider circle than his own backyard. In the midst of all this turmoil on the Clyde, Jimmy's union activities helped him to be elected as Rector of the University of Glasgow in 1971. At his installation he made a speech so powerful that it was printed in full by the *New York Times* and was said to be the "greatest speech since Lincoln's Gettysburg address". It became known as the "rat race" speech and in part he said:

> Reject the values and false morality that underlie these attitudes. A rat race is for rats. We're not rats. We're human beings. Reject the insidious pressures in society that would blunt your critical faculties to all that is happening around you, that would caution silence in the face of injustice lest you jeopardise your chances of promotion and self-advancement. This is how it starts and before you know where you are, you're a fully paid-up member of the rat-pack. The price is too high. It entails the loss of your dignity and human spirit. Or as Christ put it, "What doth it profit a man if he gain the whole world and suffer the loss of his soul?"

Jimmy was not only the master of mass meeting oratory and writer of acclaimed speeches – he could be pithy and succinct as evidenced by a remark he liked to make regularly: "The yards didn't just build ships, they built men."

Jimmy Airlie was, as mentioned, more of a strategist than Reid. He was a perfect fit for chairman of the work-in. Also a great public speaker he was an experienced negotiator, intelligent and sophisticated in his approach to union disputes. If he thought there was nothing to be obtained he was not afraid to advise against industrial action. Long-serving Labour MP Tam Dalyell said of him: "For any MP who saw him in action with employers who planned to close a factory in his constituency, he was a marvellous sight in full flow." Both Reid and Airlie had been born on the banks of the Clyde; Reid in Govan, and Airlie in Renfrew. Airlie cast a longer shadow in the union world. A former fitter he had been on the Amalgamated Engineering Union national executive since the early seventies and was involved in many other bitter union disputes, notably those involving Caterpillar, Timex and the Ford Motor Company. Tributes flowed when he died tragically early in 1997 just into his sixties. The then shadow chancellor Gordon Brown was among those at his funeral – as well as Jimmy Reid, Sammy Gilmore and Sammy Barr. The talk at the wake over "refreshments" would have been marvellous to hear.

In the seventies Jimmy Reid left the Communist Party and joined the Labour Party, but this sort of political work was not for him and he forged a new career becoming one of Scotland's most notable journalists. He even won a BAFTA award for documentaries on the USSR and had his own TV chat show. Latterly disillusion with Blair's New Labour set in and in the 2004 SNP leadership race he backed the winning team of Alex Salmond and Nicola Sturgeon, joining the party a year later. His health failing, he retired to Rothesay on Bute and died in 2010. His funeral was attended by among others Ed Balls, Ed Miliband, Gordon Brown and Alex Salmond.

The legacy of the work-in is still open to much different analysis. But its leaders could take credit for at least saving several yards despite UCS itself being put into liquidation. The receivership came in 1971 when the consortium was still making losses. Yarrow's had remained in the black, but had left the company the previous year. There is bitter memory on the Clyde that Edward Heath's Tory government announced a policy that was to end state support for what it called "lame duck" industries. This created a crisis of confidence in UCS supporters and brought on massive cash flow problems. The company had a full order book and was forecasting a profit the next year. But UCS was refused a £6 million working capital loan from the government and that was that.

Six million was a small amount to ask. It is hard to believe it was so cruelly refused and that the next year Heath relented and restructured the yards around two new commercial entities, Govan Shipbuilders (formerly Fairfield's) and Scotstoun Marine (formerly Charles Connell & Company). Brown's at Clydebank was sold to Marathon Oil to make oil rigs but that closed in 2001. The end of UCS had meant the demise of Alexander Stephens & Sons. Yarrow's carried on as an independent from 1971 to 1977 when it was nationalised as part of British Shipbuilders along with Govan Shipbuilders. The cards had been thrown in the air to fall where they could and the result was the former Fairfield's and Yarrow's at least still building under the BAE Surface Ships umbrella, concentrating on new high-tech vessels for the British and other navies. A sad and messy end to the dream of Reid, Airlie and their followers of saving all the upper Clyde yards.

20

The Flitting to End All Flittings and Surgical Success

Charting a safe passage through the name changes and various ownerships of the Clyde yards is a complex business, the sort of job an old news editor of mine liked to call "knitting with spaghetti". None more so than in the case of Yarrow's. That story began 500 or so miles south of its long-term base in Scotstoun – in Poplar in London in 1865. The founder Alfred (later Sir Alfred) moved in a couple of years to a new yard called London Yard, Cubitt Town. The connection between Yarrow and the Royal Navy is long and is still there today though now under new owners. It started in London when the Royal Navy's first destroyers known as the Havock class were built there. As in the Clyde, the shipbuilders down south were often involved in other developments, such as engines and boilers as the age of steam arrived. In London, Yarrow patented a new type of water-tube boiler, which was used in other industries as well as shipbuilding. It even helped power the London and North Eastern Railway's W1 locomotives.

By the turn of the last century it was becoming clear that

the firm was outgrowing the site. To expand in London would have been financially difficult due to the high cost of land and labour in the English capital. A bold decision was taken to move north to what we would now call a "green-field" site in Scotstoun only a few miles from the centre of Glasgow. It was a flitting to end all flittings . . . almost 5,000 tons of materials, ship models, machine tools and other engineering bits and pieces had to be moved. Trainloads of forty to fifty wagons steamed out of London heading north for days on end to accomplish it. The first ship launched in the yard in 1908, slipped down the greased ways, was, aptly considering the future of the yard, a destroyer for the Brazilian Navy.

Not far from Scotstoun, on the south bank of the river, lies the famous and imposing Erskine Hospital built to care for ex-servicemen injured in the First World War. The number of military and naval men who had lost limbs was tragically high. At this time Britain was dependant on artificial limbs manufactured abroad. One of Scotland's top surgeons of the time Sir William McEwan who worked at the hospital thought this was intolerable. He had workshops built at Erskine and he enlisted the help of Yarrow's to produce limbs. The yard put some of their best craftsmen to work designing and producing a new limb known as the Erskine Artificial Limb, which was an outstanding success. The facts speak for themselves: by the end of 1917, 1,126 limbs had been manufactured and fitted. By 1920 the figure was an astonishing almost 10,000. Despite the irony in a firm specialising in warship production playing such a role, this was a major success.

The yard in its early days was not purely a warship producer, though it did build vessels for in addition to the Brazilian Navy, the Chilean and Indian Navies. As mentioned earlier, a speciality developed in building shallow draft vessels for lakes and rivers in South America, Burma, India and other far-flung areas. Many merchant ships were also produced. And warships. In the years after the Second World War the nearby yard of the Blythswood Shipbuilding Company was bought and the land acquired used to erect covered building berths and, with the aid of a government grant, new technical offices. This facilitated the building of much of the Royal Navy's post-war fleet of destroyers and frigates. In 1985 Margaret Thatcher's thrust for industrial privatisation saw British Shipbuilders divest itself of Yarrow's, selling it to GEC-Marconi and eventually it was sold on to the marine division of BAE Systems.

Sir Eric Yarrow of the founding family joined the business in 1946 after a career as a major in the Royal Engineers. He was president of Yarrow's PLC until 1987. He was a major player in the financial and industrial scene in the West of Scotland serving six years as chairman of the Clydesdale Bank. His astuteness as a shipbuilder and banker meant that he was featured with great regularity in the broadsheet papers while his many charitable activities meant almost as many appearances in the social diary pages of the tabloids. Sir Eric had inherited his position at the top following the footsteps of his father and grandfather. One of his successors, Sir Robert Easton, had a trickier climb to the top of the greasy pole to success. Like his union opponents across the boardroom tables, Jimmy Reid and Jimmy Airlie, Easton was born on the banks of the Clyde.

Easton was an old boy of Glasgow's world-famous Royal Technical College and began his career in Govan's Fairfield's as an apprentice. In 1951 he moved to Yarrow's and worked his way up from estimator to sales director and on to managing director and chairman. Yarrow's had great strengths in the home market but the changes sweeping shipbuilding worldwide meant that his contacts in the world market and ability to sell a project were vital. Like Sir Eric he was not content to use his talents in shipping – in his career he was also a director of the Glasgow Development Agency, the West of Scotland Water Authority and Chancellor of the University of Paisley. And as Sir Eric had followed his forebears into the yard, the name Easton was kept in the fore by his son Murray who became director of BAE Systems in Scotstoun.

In recent years the sight of the latest Type 45 destroyers with their futuristic silhouette being fitted out at Yarrow's caught the eye of those travelling on the Clyde, particularly the folk enjoying a trip "doon the watter" on the *Waverley*. From 2006 the progress of *HMS Daring*, *HMS Dauntless*, *HMS Diamond*, *HMS Dragon*, *HMS Defender* and *HMS Duncan* was watched with pride. The old river could still turn out the spectacular. And these destroyers were for years a regular sight doing trials on the Firth of Clyde.

As is the case these days, the hulls and final fitting out could take place in different yards. I remember watching the launch of a Type 45 destroyer at the BAE Systems facility at the old Fairfield's Govan yard. It was impressive and memorable, hundreds of local school kids and yard workers and their families and friends cheered as the sleek state-of-the-art warship slowly gathered speed as it slipped down the greased track into the muddy waters of the Clyde. As a contrast to the grey of the ship and the brown of the river the *Waverley*, in its colourful livery, and a full load of passengers enjoying the event, sailed past in the background. The actual breaking of the champagne on the bows and the pressing of the button was conducted by the wife of a high-ranking Admiralty officer. But the ceremony was not without humour. The destroyer did not budge for a moment or two after the signal was given for it to be released. It looked as if it could be an embarrassing moment. Some of those on the launch platform even leaned forward to give the ship a helping hand on its way. But, oh so slowly, it started to move and all was well. Easy to see how it was fun to christen a ship and send her out to the oceans, especially, if unlike the Queen, it was not the sort of thing you do with any regularity.

So I was amused to read recently in a London newspaper that Tom Bower's new biography of Tony Blair reveals that Cherie Blair once asked Admiral Alan West if she could personally launch a ship. The old salt was not impressed. It seems that he was a touch miffed that he had never been asked to a Downing Street social event and grumbled that if he had been in a pop group it might have been different. Seems there was a chip on his shoulder mixed in with the gold braid. But the navy knew how to fight back. The admiral told the then PM's wife she could launch the twelfth Type 45 her husband had commissioned. He failed to mention however that Blair was about to cut the order from twelve destroyers to eight. So no Cherie on the red-and-white launch platform with bottle of bubbly to hand. That's shipbuilding business!

21

Splashing Paddles, Steam and Happy Days "Doon The Watter"

Most of the yards and the ships that created the legend Clydebuilt were in fact actual physical giants, yards that employed thousands of craftsmen and the product of their labours were super tankers, luxurious liners and huge container ships. But there is another side to this maritime story – the little ships that served the towns and villages up and down the Clyde and its firth in the days before road and rail made access easy. Vital links for the transport of goods, they were also an escape from the confines of the big cities and towns, and their smoky work-filled environments, for thousands at a time when jetting off to beaches in Florida or Spain was a distant dream. Collectively known as the Clyde Steamers these jaunty little vessels carried more than cargo, they took hard working folk out to enjoy the seascapes and mountains on the doorstep of the grimy centres of the industrial lowlands.

It might just have been a few hours' sunset sail from Dunoon or Largs or maybe a longer voyage for a fortnight's holiday in Campbeltown or Girvan. One ploy was a day trip from Glasgow to Gourock by train and then on to the steamer to Campbeltown via Lochranza. Finally moored around lunchtime at the pier in the "wee toon", as the locals call it, the passengers decamped on to the small gauge railway that ran to the lovely beach at Machrihanish and a dip in the Atlantic. Then back to Campbeltown and home for tea. It was a "public transport" trip you could not duplicate today and a memory-building experience for men and women who spent most of the year at a factory bench, sweating in a steelworks or chained to a sewing machine. For a few hours they could listen to jaunty music of the ship's band of strolling musicians, have a drink in a well-furnished saloon or maybe just breathe in the fresh sea air. These little ships became legends locked in the memories of Clydesiders.

Everyone had a favourite. Their names resonate in the Clydeside bars to this day. The story of one such vessel, the *Lucy Ashton*, spans from the nineteenth century when there was shipbuilding as far up the Clyde as Rutherglen, now a douce suburb of Glasgow, but originally a proud little town on the banks of the Clyde where the proliferation of coal fires used by its residents made its "wee red lums" famous to, remarkably, the jet age. The *Lucy Ashton* took her name from a character in Walter Scott's *The Bride of Lammermoor* and even today the evocative postcards – in her heyday as a London and North Eastern Railway steamer she was a bestseller in this popular pre-email form of communication – are remarkable for showing her style and elegance. She was built by T. B. Seath & Co, a small Rutherglen yard, now obscured by the memory of the big names downriver, in May 1888, and weighed in at a mere 271 tons. But they built them well in those days and her life on the Firth of Clyde lasted more than sixty years. She stayed on the Clyde during both world wars, unlike most of her contemporaries who were requisitioned to help with the war effort. She latched on to any pier large enough to take a rope from her. Take a scenic drive round the sea lochs of the Clyde and many of the names of her destinations are familiar, but there is no sign now of most of those piers; the wood of decks has rotted and the iron structures themselves now rust under water. The list of her regular calls is impressive – Helensburgh, Rhu, Rosneath, Clynder, Shandon, Rahane, Mambeg, Craigendoran.

Her Ruglen (as Glaswegians would render it) builders must have been very proud of her long service, which ended in 1949 when she made a final voyage to the famous Faslane shipbreakers Metal Industries. Paddle wheels, saloons, engines, superstructure were all torn out leaving only a sad-looking hull without a hint of her glory days cruising the Firth of Clyde. But surprisingly she still had history to make. The venerable old paddle steamer was to become a pioneer of the jet age. A couple of years later, after Faslane had got to work on her, the British Shipbuilding Research Association fitted four Rolls Royce jet engines on to the virtually empty hull for experiments into drag and friction on jet-powered ships.

The result was the noisiest vessel ever to sail these waters. The screaming of the four Derwent V engines was a nightmare for folk living in the vicinity. The noise was such that special sound-proofing had to be fitted to protect the ears of the researchers on board. It was a sound barrier of sorts that convinced the locals, correctly, that clamping jet engines on the decks of ships was unlikely to be a commercial success. Interestingly the noise of early hovercraft trials on the Clyde also brought experiments in this type of vessel to an end. The jet-powered *Lucy* was no Concorde and its speed was said merely to be above 15 knots. Modern visitors to the fine railway museum at York can see the carved wooden crest from her paddle box, a fitting reminder of this remarkable ship and her days owned by the London and North Eastern Railway. There was a lot of innovation going on in the great days of the Clyde steamers. *Talisman*, named after the Scott novel, is another example. This was the world's first diesel-electric paddle vessel when it was built in 1935 by A. & J. Inglis who also produced the *Waverley* (naming ships after Scott's works was quite a fashion, as mentioned). Clyde folk though remember her best not for innovation, but for her fourteen years of service on the run to Millport, that pleasant little island off Largs so popular for day trips and holiday homes for well-heeled Glaswegians.

The new engines were ahead of their time, however, and gave considerable trouble. She even had to be withdrawn from service at the peak of the 1939 holiday season. But the problems in this area did not stop her giving stalwart war service after being requisitioned by the Admiralty and temporally renamed *HMS Aristocrat* and used for anti-aircraft duties down south. The wartime name was apt as *Talisman* had always stood out from the crowd as a Clyde steamer, her single high funnel catching the eye. For years she was based at Craigendoran sailing to Dunoon and Rothesay and round the Kyles of Bute. Despite the noise and vibration of her pioneering engines she was popular with holidaymakers and carved out a high place on the list of most remembered Clyde steamers.

The arrival of modern car ferries signalled the end of the great era of Clyde steamers and by the sixties, there were only four paddlers left: *Talisman, Caledonia, Waverley* and *Jeanie Deans*. The latter was specially designed to operate out of Craigendoran for the London and North East Railway company. The versatility of the Clyde yards is demonstrated by the fact that she was built at Fairfield's upriver at Govan, the little vessel slotted in between the construction of mighty naval vessels and such as the beautiful Empress liners.

The last of this quartet of legendary paddlers was *Caledonia*, not so well remembered as the others but a ship seen by more folk than any other Clyde steamer thanks to her inglorious end. She had been built in the mid-thirties by Denny at Dumbarton and worked hard for many years out of Wemyss Bay transporting Glaswegians on holiday trips to Rothesay or Dunoon. She was another Clydebuilt vessel to be requisitioned by the navy in the Second World War and named *HMS Goatfell* for the duration. It was an apt name for a ship that spent much of her life sailing in the shadow of Arran's famous mountain. After the war she returned to the Clyde, replacing *Jeanie Deans* in the sixties before facing redundancy as the car ferries took over. She ended up as a pub called "Old Caledonia" moored at Victoria Embankment in central London, a far cry from life on the Firth of Clyde. I suspect that few of the thousands of southerners downing hot, mild beer in this reincarnation gave a thought to the fresh sea air of the *Caledonia*'s natural habitat up north. The pub/paddler closed its doors after a fire in 1980 damaged it beyond repair. For a spell it was replaced by the turbine steamer *Queen Mary II*, but like the paddlers it too had run out of profitable life up north. This Clyde steamer was originally just plain *Queen Mary* until the great Cunarder was launched and her operators agreed to bow the knee to big money and the first became the second.

Many writers on the history of the Clyde steamers make mention of the exciting business of the ships "racing for the piers". At the height of holidays "doon the watter" a great number of piers were in use, many of them today are mere lumps of rusting iron. A classic example is Arrochar pier built in 1850. Archive photographs show how popular it was with, on occasion, four steamers tied to it at one time. No doubt some of the hundreds of passengers on the vessels were enjoying the famous service the "Three Lochs Tour" which took day-trippers down the Clyde to Loch Goil and Loch Long. From there they disembarked to take a coach from Arrochar the few miles west to Tarbet on Loch Lomond and then took another steamer trip up the legendary loch. This particular pier is now derelict, after the tourist traffic declined after the world wars and a storm in the 1970s damaged it.

Incidentally, Arrochar unlike some of the tourist piers was also used by cargo vessels with coal from Glasgow and Ireland. Wool from the thousands of sheep grazing the hills across the loch from the pier was also sent down to Liverpool from this pier. As in the case of Arrochar many of the passenger services to Clyde piers were operated by railway companies who were in intense competition with each other, not just on Loch Long, but up and down the Clyde. The piers, particularly Craigendoran, and Dunoon were often buzzing with sightseers and potential passengers. If a couple of ships were approaching a pier it was important to arrive there first to scoop up the fares. And skippers often took risks to be a winner. Many accidents resulted, though fortunately without much loss of life, though there were fatalities recorded when steamers ran down yachts or small sightseeing vessels in crowded waters around the most popular resort piers. One of the "Bibles" of the fraternity who have followed the goings-on in the Clyde down the years is Alan J. S. Paterson's *The Golden Years of the Clyde Steamers* (1889–1914), a hugely informative and entertaining book. In it he gives a vivid account of the potential danger of racing for the piers.

The two ships involved in a spectacular collision in 1899 both had legendary Clyde names that were used on several vessels over the years and are familiar to steamer buffs – the *Marchioness of Lorne* and the *Glen Sannox*. The *Glen Sannox* had been launched in 1892 and had earned a deserved reputation as a flier, often used on the Ardrossan–Arran route. Its builder was J. & G. Thomson who had a yard in the Cessnock district of Glasgow before moving downriver to a site on the north bank of the river at Barns O'Clyde near Dalmuir, the village that was to become known as Clydebank. Thomson's was bought by John Brown's at the start of the famous yard's rise to worldwide fame. The rival of the *Glen Sannox* had an equally impressive pedigree. The *Marchioness of Lorne* came from the Port Glasgow yard of William Russell mostly famous as the builders of the elegant full-rigged *Falls of Clyde*. This yard eventually came under the umbrella of Lithgow's.

By 1899 these two thoroughbreds were in competition on the summer Arran run, the *Glen Sannox* owned by the Glasgow and South Western Railway and the *Marchioness* by the Caledonian company. On a fine June day with the Firth of Clyde looking its sparkling best the *Marchioness* was the first to leave Brodick bound for the railhead at Ardrossan. Twelve minutes later she was followed by the *Glen Sannox* who, living up to her reputation as a speed merchant, caught up with her rival on the approach to the narrow entrance to the Ayrshire harbour, still a dangerous place in bad weather. But the master of the *Marchioness* was in no mood to be overtaken and in the nautical equivalent of road rage deliberately steered his ship on a course to foil the faster ship. A collision was inevitable and both vessels were badly damaged though there was no loss of life.

Also inevitable was a Board of Trade Inquiry into this

dangerous farce. The result of this seems to the modern eye hard to believe. Clearly the men to blame were Captain McGregor of the *Glen Sannox* and the temporary master of the *Marchioness*, a Mr McMillan. They were both censured, but despite the court issuing a strong warning against the practice of "racing" their certificates were not suspended and they were free to sail again! This was just one incident on crowded waters that could have ended in tragedy. Later races to the piers might not have been so reckless, but they continued for years. Old Clyde hands tell of crowds on Dunoon pier in particular watching with enjoyment as paddlers from Craigendoran on the north bank and Gourock on the south vied to be first to reach the resort.

At the risk of being accused of self-indulgence I end this chapter with my favourite Clyde steamer, the *Duchess of Hamilton*. The reason is simple – I spent many happy hours on it travelling to our second hometown of Campbeltown. It was fast and beautiful. Seeing it moored at Gourock waiting for the passengers to descend from the Glasgow train and take the short walk to join the ship, I knew that at last the long awaited summer holidays had really started. The regular run to "the wee town" passed quickly and the final miles down the Kilbrannan Sound from Lochranza were exciting with every chance of seeing a basking shark. Something you can still do today though the car ferry from Lochranza to Claonaig can't match the old *Duchess* for glamour.

22

Little Giants Anchored in Clydeside Memory

It is one of the first memories I have of the Clyde – the puffers. For much of the last century these small, usually coal-fired, cargo ships were a much loved part of the west-coast scene. They are now almost completely gone, sadly before the days of satellite navigation arrived. Anoraks, like myself, these days spend a lot of time sitting at home gazing at websites on laptops that track the movement of ships, large and small, worldwide, zeroing in on the Firth of Clyde. There is fascination in watching the little icons representing the different types of vessel float across the screen as they go about their business, particularly fishing boats from the likes of Carradale, Girvan, Campbeltown, Dunure and Tarbert, hunting for any white fish left and prawns and scallops in the areas where such tasty culinary treats have not been dredged out of existence by over fishing. Or checking that Western Ferries and CalMac are keeping to time as they plough the firth transporting tourists, commuters, cargoes, cars and lorries to their destinations. There is, too, the chance of watching a larger than normal icon appear on screen as one of the growing number of large cruise ships visiting the Clyde moves around the lochs and islands. For the rest, it is usually watching a dwindling number of smallish cargo vessels or the occasional super tanker or container ship and naval movements. How much more interesting to have been able to plot the movements of the puffers. The pleasure of following puffers on a flickering screen was never to be. And these days you can generally only see one puffer making its way around the firth – the *VIC 32*, converted into a mini cruise boat, operating out of Crinan, with passenger numbers in tens rather than thousands. Apart from this much-loved relic of different days, two vessels which dodged the breaker's yard can still give enthusiasts a flavour of what life on a puffer was like but without the chance to actually go to sea. Another ageing VIC is moored at Inveraray not far from the birthplace of Neil Munro, author of the marvellous *Para Handy* short stories of puffer life. And the puffer *Spartan* is on display at the Scottish Maritime Museum.

Neil Munro is unchallenged as the man who has done most to burn the history of puffers into the collective Scottish memory. Munro was one of the pre-eminent newspapermen of his day, successful in both his journalism and his novel writing. The tales of the *Vital Spark* and its crew, as they wandered around the West Coast, first appeared in the now defunct *Glasgow Evening News* in 1905. For Munro they were, as Para Handy himself might have said, a "diversion" from his serious newspaper work. Indeed he used the pen name Hugh Foulis for them in order that this basically humorous writing did not detract from his more serious novels. I suspect that when he penned his first *Para Handy* story he would have been surprised to know that the characters were to appear in the newspaper for more than twenty years. And to find that they inspired three BBC television series, the last in 1995. (The puffer, too, had a moment of cinema fame in a charming little movie, *The Maggie,* made in the fifties starring Hollywood actor Paul Douglas.) It is ironic that Munro is mostly more remembered for *Para Handy* than anything else he wrote. Incidentally the puffers were so familiar to his readers in his Glasgow paper that he gives little space to describing their appearance or history. The magic is in the humour of his characters but underneath the amusement provided by their adventures, such as a spot of illegal splash netting at the mouth of a salmon river or high jinks in harbour-side hostelries, lies a deep insight into the human nature of the puffer fraternity, their families and backgrounds and the folk they rubbed up against on their gentle travels round the Firth of Clyde.

The history of the puffers themselves is fascinating. The origin of the very name puffer was largely forgotten by the time the vessels were in their heyday. The original puffer is considered by many experts to be the *Thomas* built as long ago as 1856. The engine was a very simple steam one and since the *Thomas* and other early vessels spent most of their time on canals, with plenty of fresh water available, a condenser was not necessary to economise in water use. This meant that after moving the piston the steam was simply vented up the funnel making a character "puffing" noise. The background of canal work also had other effects on the design. The size was constricted to less than 66 feet to allow the vessel to fit the Forth and Clyde Canal locks. The bluff bows so typical of the type maximised the hold space. The hull of a puffer is often said to be flat bottomed though that was not strictly true, but it was flat enough to enable beaching. And a flat bottom, not much help in some types of weather, was nevertheless important to allow unloading in remote areas with no piers, but suitable firm sandy beaches that allowed lorries and carts to come alongside. The danger here was that the boat might settle on some unseen rock and perhaps break its back. Holidaymakers to the Clyde resorts are well aware that long "sandy" beaches often have the odd small but sharp rock peppered about and a danger to any youngster out for a dip in the mostly icy waters. Many of the old puffer skippers had a good working knowledge of where such danger lay, often carrying their own marked charts.

Para Handy himself, who always claimed that the *Vital Spark* was the "smertest boat in the trade" and often dipped into his own pockets to give her a lick of paint when needed, had a dislike of dirty cargoes. But for puffer owners it mattered not whether coal or gravel or the assorted jumble of a Highland farm flitting filled the hold, provided the price was right. In the opening short story Para Handy's deep feelings for his vessel are expressed thus:

> Oh man! She was the beauty! She was just sublime! She should be carryin' nothing but gentry for passengers, or nice genteel luggage for the shooting lodges, but there they would be spoiling her and rubbing all the pent off her with their coals, and sand, and whunstone and oak bark and timber and trash like that.

No complaints though about another cargo latterly much carried by some puffers – whisky from the west coast's many distilleries.

Chugging around the sheltered calm waters of the upper firth on a windless summer day could have been a pleasure rather than work, something hinted at in Munro's wonderful stories. But these sturdy little boats worked summer and winter, and trips out in the Atlantic swells to Barra or other Hebridean destinations or round the Mull of

191

Kintyre in a force nine winter gale, were another story. It would not be too much of an exaggeration to say there was a touch of Cape Horn in such a trip.

The puffers were built in growing numbers from the mid-1850s to the start of the Second World War. Voyaging further down the Firth of Clyde and out to the Hebrides required more sophisticated engines than those of the early versions, but the basics of the design and the appearance of these sturdy little ships was largely unchanged even after the arrival of diesel engines. The crew quarters were dark and often damp, lacking the comforts of even slightly larger seagoing coasters. The various television series gave the viewer some insight into crew life, with bunks, and a table forward of the hold and with the skipper having a cramped cabin in the stern. By far the best evocation of what life was like on a puffer is in Dan McDonald's splendid book *The Clyde Puffer*. Dan made several voyages by puffer in the seventies and of the crew accommodation he writes:

> In the conditions prevailing in a puffer at sea a cast iron stomach was a more valuable asset than a Board of Trade certificate. Crew accommodation consisted of a triangular space only 15 feet across lit only by the hatch and a few glass bricks let into the deck. Into this confined space was fitted a large coal fired range and water tank, four bunks in two tiers, a locker for food and crockery, a wooden stool or bench, and right in the bows the bosun's locker. The "usual offices" were housed in a small erection like a watchman's hut on the quarterdeck.

He told his readers that the puffer men supplied their own food and how vital it was that the deckhand who was caterer, cook, relief engineer and seaman as required, was up to the job. The puffer men lived in a close-knit group, all real-life characters who could have dropped into Neil Munro's stories effortlessly. Most were known by their nicknames – Handsome Harry Walker, Cocky Grey, Dublin Joe, Jock the Wrecker, The Sparrow and The Butcher being just a few. Dan McDonald's stories of annual holiday trips on the puffers are entertaining and personal, but he was also a serious historian of the vessels. He reckons that around 400 or so were built and many came from now largely forgotten yards on the Forth and Clyde Canal though even such mighty firms as Denny's built a couple for family connections. One of the most remarkable builders was John Hay at Kirkintilloch, which operated for almost 100 years. Kirkie, as the locals call it, in pastoral flatlands miles from the open sea was an unlikely location for shipbuillding but it had two yards, Hay's and that of Peter McGregor & Sons. Hay's built or operated around 100 puffers and McGregor's around twenty. The canal heritage was important to the puffer design and some were even built in a yard at Blackhill for the smallish Monkland Canal.

Even the most fantasising puffer enthusiast could hardly use the term warship in connections with these vessels that, born in canals, had grown to be familiar in the west coast resorts and commercial ports. But they played a role in both world wars. In 1914 there was the need for the Royal Navy to create new harbours at Scapa Flow and on the east coast. To service the awesome battleships and cruisers, the time-handy small vessels were needed for shore-to-ship deliveries and other tasks. During the war problems with rail transport, particularly on the west coast, meant that the navy and local communities were more dependent than ever on sea transport. The puffers were ideal for the job. Many were drafted into the support role including some that had moved north from the Forth area. In the years between the wars there was less commercial use of canals and some of the replacement puffers being built were longer than the old standard but still able to use the short cut to the Atlantic provided by the Crinan Canal. Two examples of the new puffers of the thirties were the *Glencloy* and *Sealight*. Their design was the basis of a new fleet of puffers ordered by the Ministry of War Transport. These were known as "Victualling Inshore Craft" or VICs. After the Second World War around a dozen or so of these VICs found their way back to the Clyde and were a familiar part of the scene.

The little giants were coming to the end of their lives. Rising wages and fuel costs meant the economics were against them. They had had their day. But today the affection for the puffer is still strong. The smell of the smoke and steam, the sound of the whistle, the images of those small coasters going about their business in the deep darkness of a west coast night with the occasional blast of flame from the funnel lighting up the Firth of Clyde lives on. Too many names to list but, such as *Moonlight, Starlight, Spartan, Lascar, Anzac, Roman* and *Pibroch* and many others will not be forgotten. And nor will "A short thick set man with a red beard, a hard round felt hat, ridiculously out of harmony with a blue pilot jacket, and trousers and a seaman's jersey. . ." The immortal Para Handy and the puffers together live on in Clydeside's memory.

23

A Despot, Days of Drama and a New Destiny

From Rutherglen to Gourock, from Govan to Helensburgh – for hundreds of years both banks of the Clyde have been fertile ground producing a rich, undulating history of remarkable people who made a difference to their world. Engineering innovation and imagination mixed with commercial success and, at times, with financial and human tragedy. In this final chapter there is both horror and drama from the past and hope for the future, a different future in the age of climate change. A new dream is taking root in one of the most historic areas associated with Clyde shipbuilding – Port Glasgow.

It has always struck me that one of the most attractive features of Clydeside is its diversity. Many folk think of the yards as bleak, dirty, noisy and often dangerous work-places. But the workers in the assembly sheds or engine workshops and the directors in the board rooms had one pleasure not shared by tenement dwellers in Glasgow who toiled at desks in dreary city offices. The folk in the yards could step outside for a minute or two, breath in some ozone-rich air fresh off the Atlantic and take in the view of the firth or the mountains of Argyll. And, of course, when the industry was at its peak they could take pleasure and pride in what the efforts of their hard work produced – the greatest liners of the great days of the liners, the biggest tankers and bulk carriers ever produced and mighty warships that changed the course of history.

That entire heritage is on the doorstep of the new Glasgow, a place reinvented by its time as City of Culture, now a city that is a superb tourist destination. Away from the glitter of the theatres, the fine dining in world-class restaurants, cafe society and friendly pubs, the tourist looking for a scenic drive is spoiled for choice.

One trip well worth taking is a drive from Glasgow to Gourock following the south bank of the river. It is a drive providing at times spectacular views across the Clyde and the Tail of the Bank from Lyle Hill high above Greenock. The Cloch Lighthouse, just beyond Gourock where the firth opens out, could mark the end of such a trip. It is not a spectacular lighthouse, no tall structure perched on a lonely rock miles out on open water. But this modest roadside lighthouse has been a much-loved Clyde icon for hundreds of years, a welcome sign to voyagers that they have arrived home in safe waters. And a last sight of their birthplace for Clydebuilt ships heading out for the oceans of the world.

It is almost impossible to mention Scotland and light-houses without mentioning the "Lighthouse Stevensons". Four generations of this remarkable family were involved in the building of almost every lighthouse in Scotland. Robert Louis Stevenson may have been thought prolific in the world of letters, but his family were massively prolific not with words, but with building materials and their life-saving work is to been seen around the entire coast of Scotland. The Cloch's roadside situation and design may

196

not be as spectacular as that of the iconic structure Robert Stevenson constructed on the dangerous and isolated Bell Rock many miles away off Scotland's east coast, but it is a Firth of Clyde landmark and legend. Now, of course it is unmanned and, like most of the remaining lighthouses, completely automated. If it still had a crew of keepers, no doubt they would be happy that the days when the mechanism had to be wound up by hand every three hours or so night and day were gone. The Cloch was completed in 1797 and the original oil lantern was first lit on 11 August, in time to serve as a guiding light in the coming darkness of a Scottish winter. Later, the light source was modified several times and foghorns, an ominous and mournful howl in the mists familiar to those who lived in the area, added. Today the light that shines out to passing shipping is more prosaically mounted on a pole outside the old lantern tower.

Legendary lighthouse builder Robert Stevenson co-designed the Cloch with his father-in-law Thomas Smith, engineer for the Northern Lighthouse Board. The Cloch has been much altered down the years – for generations the Stevensons were innovators not content with a standard design. They constantly introduced the latest technology of the time. The Cloch marks the entrance to the Clyde proper and also serves as a warning of the Gantocks rocks, just off Dunoon, across the channel. To get to the Cloch from Glasgow by car you have to navigate some tricky roundabouts and confusing road layouts. The trickiest of these roundabouts marks the start of Port Glasgow (though the impressive high old brown-brick building on the edge of the road at this point was confusingly known as the Gourock Rope Works!). Here the traveller meets markers of the old and new Clyde. Newark Castle is just a rivet's throw outside the gates of Ferguson's yard, and well worth a break in your journey.

If you can find the right exit on the nearby roundabout you drive into an area that has still all the bustle of a shipyard in expansion mode. Amid all the evidence of a declining past nearby, with its empty docks and rusting cranes, Ferguson's is a heartening sight for the shipbuilding enthusiast. This part of Port Glasgow is coming alive again with the demolition of aged offices and unused buildings and their replacement by modern offices and new fabrication buildings unstained by the passing of time. A new future is being built almost in the shadow of the impressive old Newark Castle. Somehow the mingling of ancient and modern seems apt. If walls could talk, as the cliché has it, the stones of Newark could tell a fascinating story of shipbuilding around the site. And human dramas. Before the construction of a new harbour at Port Glasgow, nearer to the city, the ports of the Ayrshire coast handled most of the maritime commerce in southwest Scotland. Upriver from what was to become Port Glasgow the waters narrowed and shifting sandbanks were a danger. Until the advent of dredging to take shipping into almost the centre of Glasgow itself, the site beside Newark Castle was the natural place for growth as the prosperity of Glasgow burgeoned and the Ayrshire harbours became too distant to serve the growing metropolis.

The phoenix-like renaissance of Ferguson's after years of decline and its significance in the future of industrial Scotland will bring new prominence to Newark Castle. There is plenty for the visitor, even those not attracted by the shipbuilding history, to enjoy. As you face the river the walls of the shipyard are on your left. In its heyday the castle sat surrounded by other yards. Now the area to the east has been cleared and there is a country park and walkways to enjoy as well as clear views to Dumbarton and its castle on the other bank. On a day of sunshine in such rural surroundings it is hard to imagine just how busy the industrial scene in the Port Glasgow area was. The long list of yards now closed, some forgotten almost completely, illustrates how different it must have been. The yards long gone include the now little known William Hamilton & Company who built a cargo and passenger steamer for the New York and South America Line as well as dozens of vessels for owners in far-flung corners of the globe. Others include Lamont's who were still building Clyde car ferries in the seventies and Murdoch & Murray, Russell & Company and Dunlop Bremner & Company. These days, motoring past the remnants of the old and the existing yards with the skyline full of cranes, many rusting alas, and glimpses of dry docks and derelict fitting-out yards behind high brown brick walls, is depressing. In the old days of full production it must have been awesome.

Clydeside has always seemed to have the ability to nurture remarkable characters, most of whom became famous for engineering inventions or spectacular entre-preneurship. However, there is always in history room for an exception. One such was the most infamous laird of Newark Castle, Patrick Maxwell. This despot and his story, which is still told to fascinated schoolchildren in the area, is an interesting part of the history of the area, though Patrick Maxwell does not appear to have been much of a shipbuilder himself.

The castle had been built as far back as 1478 by a George Maxwell and was much altered and rebuilt by Patrick Maxwell in the late sixteenth century when he inherited it. He is the man responsible for the fine renaissance mansion, a more accurate description than castle, that visitors admire today. There was nothing to like about the man himself. He is remembered for the fact that he murdered several of his neighbours and fathered a large number of children by his wife Margaret who he treated abominably. The despicable Maxwell regularly beat her and on one occasion confined her to her bed chamber for six months on bread and water. Even his own mother complained to the authorities about his behaviour. Some will tell you that life has always been hard for Greenock and Port Glasgow folk. That may be, but life in Newark Castle was spectacularly hard. Eventually Margaret fled across the river to find sanctuary in Dumbarton. How did the villainous Patrick get away with it? Friends in high places it seems. He was a close associate of King James VI of Scotland who kept him onside. Certainly, Patrick Maxwell was, in personality and actions, as different as it is possible to be from the others who lived around him and helped create the shipbuilding industry in Port Glasgow.

For the visitor to Newark Castle these days there is plenty to see. Modern day youngsters in particular would no doubt be particularly interested in the cellars. Here one of the later owners, a local rope maker called John Orr, kept wild animals such as big cats and bears brought to the Clyde by voyaging sailors. The inside of the castle is in remarkably good condition and gives a good idea of what life must have been like in the old days. Elderly tenement dwellers down from Glasgow or from Port Glasgow itself will recognise a feature from their own youth – a "bed press" that folded away into the walls.

The significance of, and interest in, the Newark Castle area now extends far beyond the murky past of Patrick Maxwell. There are hopes that pioneering vessels now being built at Ferguson's could spark a "green" revolution on the Clyde and lead to new business opportunities worldwide. Climate change is seldom out of the headlines today, but it is a subject fraught with complexity and competing scientific opinions. The layman mostly sees cars, diesel-powered lorries and coalmines as the main perpetrators of dangerous emissions. The huge cargo vessels and cruise ships tend to wander the oceans, often ploughing a lonely path out of sight and out of mind, without criticism. It seems counter-intuitive to blame marine transport for much of the damage to the atmosphere. It is not necessary to plunge very deeply into the scientific literature to see that this is not necessarily the case. Blue-water ships can be extreme polluters. One estimate is that the largest fifteen ships in the world emit as much nitrogen oxide and sulphur oxide into the atmosphere as millions of cars. We have a problem and one solution could be the evolution of battery power and liquid gas power for freighters, ferries, warships and the growing armada of cruise ships.

There is certain inevitability in the Clyde being a pioneer in this new field. Has the area not always, through good times and bad, been at the forefront of engineering development from the days of the *Comet* to the latest warships just ordered by the Royal Navy? The hard evidence of a renaissance is easy to see in Newark Castle's backyard where the vision of entrepreneur Jim McColl is tearing down the remnants of the old Ferguson's and replacing it with a revived and renamed state-of-the-art engineering facility called FMEL (Ferguson Marine Engineering Ltd.). The story of how we got to this point is complex. Peter Ferguson co-founded shipbuilders Fleming & Ferguson but left to strike out with his three brothers, Daniel, Louis and Robert to form a new firm simply called Ferguson and in 1903 they leased the Newark shipyard. The cost was £500 a year and the first order was for two steam tugs.

From then until the present day, changes of name and ownership seemed as regular as the Gourock–Glasgow trains that thunder past the front door. In 1918 it was bought by John Slater Ltd. but bought back by the Ferguson family in the twenties. In the fifties Lithgow's had an interest in the yard which lasted in various forms until 1977 when it became part of the nationalised British Shipbuilders (during this period it was amalgamated with the Ailsa yard in Troon). Later it was owned by Clark Kincaid and then Holland House. At the start of the new century things looked to be on the up when ninety additional jobs were created after Ferguson won a £17 million contract. The outbreak of industrial and commercial peace only lasted a few years and by 2005 the yard was back in the headlines as political warfare over the future of its jobs broke out.

Two potentially juicy contracts were available at a time when order books were low – one for a CalMac vessel and the other for a new fisheries protection vessel for the Scottish Executive. The orders went to Poland and the company furiously – and with some justification – complained that the eastern Europeans were using government subsidy to undercut the competition. It is a complaint that from time to time has also cropped up in the aviation and car-making industries. First Minister, at the time, Jack McConnell lamely said that European procurement rules didn't allow the SNP to give "preferential treatment" for Scottish ship-builders. Even a call for an investigation by the SNP was ruled out. Workers were laid off and there was real fear for the future of the yard.

Ferguson's and its workforce was on a roller coaster ride – orders from Western Ferries and their rival CalMac temporarily saved the day, but it was a crisis postponed. There were more redundancies in 2007. But in 2011 there was news that was to be a precursor of the saving of the yard. A deal to build among the world's first – a phrase so often used down the years in connection with the Clyde – hybrid (a mixture of battery power and conventional engines) ferries was won against European competition.

And in 2012 *MV Hallaig* was launched, the first commercial ship to be fully built and delivered on the Clyde for a number of years. Good news powered along with the help of more than £20 million from the Scottish government. A couple of years later a second similar ferry, *MV Lochinvar* was launched, a vessel I know well for its service on the Portavadie–Tarbert route. The pioneer *Hallaig* was among the first of a new breed and the name was chosen from a Sorley MacLean poem about an abandoned township on the island of Raasay, off Skye, and the vessel has served well on the short crossing from Sconser. Nicola Sturgeon, then Scotland's Deputy First Minister, performed the naming ceremony.

Hallaig weighs in at 135 tons and is 150 feet long with the ability to carry around 150 passengers and twenty-three cars or two large heavy goods vehicles, much needed to transport major loads to a relatively remote island. The Ro-Ro hybrid uses a low carbon emission system of diesel electric power and lithium ion battery power. Like such cars as the Nissan Leaf and others it can be plugged in and recharged overnight, an ideal solution for vessels that only operate in the daylight hours on short crossings. Like much that has happened in recent years in Ferguson's, the commissioning of *Hallaig* was not without problems. Late changes in fire safety regulations meant that both she and *Lochinvar* had to have unplanned extensive work done to allow insulation to be fitted to exposed steel and aluminium.

Not long after the *Hallaig* went into service there was a huge shock to come for the workers at the yard. They turned up one August morning to find the company had gone bust and seventy employees were made redundant on the spot. Over the years there has been much political talk, some of it true, of irresponsible shipyard unions and their work practices. But in the modern world, surely to treat a workforce this way was outrageous. A union repre-sentative, Alex Logan, said: "We are shocked and stunned. We've had an idea since before the summer that something was going on but have been unable to get any information from the management. We thought that maybe the yard was going to be sold, but there was no indication that it was going to close."

Then along came the wealthy entrepreneur Jim McColl. He joined the pantheon of that impressive list of men who ruled and saved Clyde yards before him. It was a case of the right man in the right place at the right time. Born in Carmunnock, on the southern edge of Glasgow, he left school at sixteen to start an engineering apprenticeship with the world famous Weir Pumps in Cathcart, just a few miles down the road from his home village. His rise to the top was truly spectacular. By middle age his CV could list dozens of awards in a career as a company doctor taking large businesses out of financial turbulence and huge losses back into profit. He didn't just do it once, it has happened again and again. The turnaround most associated with him is that of Clyde Blowers Capital, which now has a turnover of almost a billion and a half and employs more than 5,000 people round the world. In one of those delightful twists of fate they bought Weir Group in 2007. I wonder if the youngster who walked through the massive doors of the factory, just off Clarkston Road in Glasgow, thought such a thing would ever happen.

Or that in 2014 he would be able to rescue Ferguson's from death. But "Mr Turnaround" or the "Resurrection Man" as some papers call him did just that. The hustle and bustle around the yard in the "garden" of Newark Castle is there for everyone to see, whether from the nearby Glasgow–Gourock road, or a close-up on a downriver cruise on the *Waverley*. If plucking the yard from the ashes was good news, even better was to come – in September 2015 it was announced that Ferguson Marine Engineering was the preferred bidder for a £97 million bid to build two ferries. This secured the jobs of the existing workers and promised more expansion in the future.

According to CalMac the ferries will be "dual-fuel" vessels able to operate on liquefied natural gas (LNG) and marine diesel. LNG is significantly less damaging to the atmosphere and has been adopted by ferry operators in northern Europe in response to tighter emissions regulations. The ships are designed to carry 127 cars or sixteen HGVs or a combination of both and hundreds of passengers. The ships will be capable of operating across a range of draughts and speeds to meet the requirements of the current operator, CalMac Ferries Ltd, to service a wide range of ports and routes.

It is good to be able to close my "Song of the Clyde" on an optimistic note. Upriver from Ferguson's the two BAE yards – on the old Yarrow's site and in Govan – have been promised Royal Navy warship building work that could take production into the 2030s. All this is pleasant to reflect upon on a spring day heading for the beauty of Argyll. Waiting for *Lochinvar* to come across silently (those batteries!) from Tarbert to pick us up, it occurs to me that I am waiting for more than a ferry. That blink of sunlight splashing on the white superstructure a mile or so away, across a smooth Loch Fyne, could just be the future.

Selected Sources and Suggested Further Reading

Books:

Conley, Dan and Richard Woodman (2014), *Cold War Command*, Seaforth Publishing

Craig, Gavin (1971), *Boy Aloft*, Nautical Publishing Company

Cunard (2011), *Cunard Queens*

Duckworth, Christian and Graham Langmuir (1972), *Clyde River and Other Steamers*, Brown, Son & Ferguson Ltd

Flannery, Tim (2000), *The Life and Adventures of John Nicol, Mariner*, Canongate

Frost, Jack & Neil Potter (1969), *Queen Elizabeth 2: The Authorised Story*, George G. Harrap & Co. Ltd.

Hennessy, Peter and James Jinks (2015), *The Silent Deep*, Allen Lane

Large, Captain Vincent (1971), *Windjammer 'Prentice*, Jerrold's

Larson, Erik (2015), *Dead Wake: The Last Crossing of the Lusitania*, Transworld

McDonald, Dan (1994), *The Clyde Puffer*, Thomas & Lochar

McGinn, Keith, *Last of the Puffermen*, Neil Wilson Publishing

Munro, Neil, illustrated by Hamish Haswell-Smith (2003), *The Vital Spark*, Black & White Publishing

Osborne, Brian D., Iain Quinn and Donald Robertson (1996), *Glasgow's River*, Lindsay Publications

Paterson, Alan J. S. (2001), *The Golden Age of the Clyde Steamers* (1889-1914), Newton Abbot, David and Charles

Ransford, Oliver (1967), *Livingstone's Lake*, Thomas Y Crowell

Sherry, Alan (1996), *The Blackburn – Dumbarton's Aircraft Factory*, Stenlake Publishing

Small, Sam (2008), *Greater Glasgow: An Illustrated Architectural Guide*, Rutland Press

Villiers, Alan (1930), *By Way of Cape Horn*, Hodder and Stoughton

Willasey-Wilsey, Tim, *The Irrawaddy*

Newspapers:
Daily Record
The Daily Telegraph
Greenock Telegraph
The Guardian
The Herald
The National
The Scotsman

Other Sources:
Clydebuilt Ships database
Denny Ship Tank Museum, Dumbarton
Famous Ships of the Clyde (Glasgow Royal Concert Hall, 1993)
Scottish Engineering Hall of Fame, engineeringhalloffame.org.uk
Scottish Maritime Museum, Irvine

Index

Ships

Yards